LOUISIANA
IN WORDS

LOUISIANA IN WORDS

EDITED BY JOSHUA CLARK

PELICAN PUBLISHING COMPANY

Gretna 2007

*The word "Pelican" and the depiction of a pelican are trademarks
of Pelican Publishing Company, Inc., and are registered in the
U.S. Patent and Trademark Office.*

Library of Congress Cataloging-in-Publication Data

Louisiana in words / edited by Joshua Clark.
        p. cm.
    Includes index.
    ISBN 978-1-58980-429-6 (pbk. : alk. paper)
    1. Louisiana — Description and travel — Anecdotes. 2. Louisiana —
Social life and customs — Anecdotes. 3. Louisiana — History, Local —
Anecdotes. 4. Louisiana — Biography — Anecdotes. I. Clark, Joshua,
1975-
    F376.L683 2007
    976.3'064 — dc22

                                        2006038392

Barry Gifford's "8:00 p.m." has been adapted from the original and
used by permission of the author.

John Biguenet's "6:36 a.m." previously appeared in slightly different form in *The New Orleans Review.*

Printed in the United States of America

Published by Pelican Publishing Company, Inc.
1000 Burmaster Street, Gretna, Louisiana 70053

INTRODUCTION

4:33 A.M.

IT'S DIFFICULT FOR HIM TO SEE Louisiana in it anymore. The red highways have become arteries, the slight blue curves of rivers veins, the levels of brown contour intervals like fine wrinkles, the skin blotched with cities like graying bruises. Then, in the map's very bottom right corner the blue of the Gulf becomes dark, so dark the depth it conveys frightens him. It seems as though this is where the foot is headed, where it will scrape off the muck hanging from its sole—the southern parishes built of swamp, from New Orleans to New Iberia.

It's next to his bed, the only thing he has on his bedroom walls. It's about three feet tall and wide and, thanks to the United States Geological Survey, contains the most accurate geographical information humanly possible of our state, our state alone.

For years now, when sleep will not come, he has traveled around and around the state with his eyes, wondering what people are doing, dreaming right then in all those pinprick black dots joined by the crooked red roads thin as hair. He imagines the people there on his map, about the size of atoms, living their days, moving in circles, alone and together, bumping into one another in patternless rhythm. He wants to know them, these places, with more than his fingertip. He wants to grow them to life-size proportions, hear them, feel their light, smell their seasons, taste their waters, know them so well they in turn know him.

And so he has tried in the past years to touch as many of these places as possible, driven through them, slept in them, listened to them, ate, drank and breathed in them, but they are too many, and there is too little time for anything but a fleeting grasp at them, never any real hold, and never time enough for them to hold him.

Now, this morning, below the framed map are seven boxes piled

5

high with words telling him exactly what is happening in virtually every one of those dots, on every contour, every bayou, river, and lake. And so begins the long process of culling through submissions for *Louisiana in Words*. In these boxes, now in this book, are true stories, voices of generations, life and death, joy and sorrow, man and nature inside our state's borders.

After *America 24/7* was published, so was a similar book for every state. Like others before them, done the world over, these "day in the life" books, while necessary and remarkable in their own way, were mostly photographs. A picture can say a thousand words—an expression someone had to put into words, of course—but the right words can portray a million pictures, ones far more complex and meaningful than can ever be caught through the photographer's lens and squashed onto a silver halide negative or megabytes of pixels. Never before had a book sought to capture a single day in a state through short written pieces by different writers. Would it work?

Writing a true minute so that others can feel it, getting in so close they become a new person for a page, is quite different from snapping a photograph from a distance. Anyone can point a camera, take a thousand images, capture one that speaks to us—but to form a thousand words that brought together ring truth, to only have one shot?

Calls for submissions went out to every newspaper in the state (who knew we had well over a hundred?) and every public library, college, Web site, writing group, radio station, you name it, as well as international writing publications. The basic guidelines were fairly simple: In one page or less, write about one minute, anytime, anywhere in Louisiana. The response, in both quality and quantity, was tremendous, and many worthy pieces had to be excluded.

Though hurricanes inextricably frame our views of the world now, we asked that submissions not focus on them. Those minutes will continue to be told elsewhere. The words "Katrina" and "Rita" do not appear in a single story, yet some of these works presage not only the floods—such as the second piece—but the hope with which we've met our greatest challenge.

The stories' themes reveal our state in all its simplicity and complexity. And the writers range from MFA professors to people putting pencil to paper for the first time since grade school (and one who is in grade school).

Selecting the best writing would have been too easy. Selecting writing that best conveys the spirits of our state is another matter. Many didn't know how to write their first story any other way than to simply tell it. Their style is bare because there is none. And their every word wrenches truth from their minute.

There is no time to blink when you read these pieces. You might miss the magic. Some minutes are written after decades of intimate knowledge of a subject; others depict something their writers observed only briefly, something they will never see again. But all are firsthand observations. Many of the pieces are autobiographical, yet most writers refer to themselves as we would — in the third person.

There are conflicting perspectives on these pages, some that many people will not agree with, yet it would be dishonest to our state's nature to exclude them. As everywhere, ignorance rears its head in our state, and it will be shown here. And too, these pieces are not free of other "faults" that buck trends of modern literature. For instance, there's plenty of sentimentality, but only when the sentiment is honest to the story's, and state's, nature, rather than a romanticized notion of our place in the world.

The pieces run chronologically from dawn to dawn, spanning one single day, any day, merging past and present. They range from frost to swelter, from a man telling the story behind a picture of him taken in 1926 to the present day. Change and preservation, hand in hand, sweep across these pages beneath fleeting strokes of sun and sister stars. They are testament to what was, is, and always will be.

Of course, we cannot exhaust every last element of our state between these covers. But together these minutes provide a mosaic that conveys a whole Louisiana to the disparate regions within our state, to the outside world, and to the future.

A minute. The time it takes to defrost a couple of slices of bread in the microwave. The time it takes for your $200 high heels to sink into the mud around your mother's grave. The time it takes an old yardman whose name you never knew to save your young daughter from being kidnapped. Time it takes a levee to rupture. Teach your grandchildren to listen to the giant live oaks beneath which you grew up. To learn hate from men in white hoods. To bury a sparrow in the Mississippi.

And so he stands in his bedroom, facing the map on his wall, 4:33 a.m., above these pages, these words stacked below him. Now they are yours, ours.

—*Joshua Clark*

LOUISIANA
IN WORDS

Benton•

Caddo•

Dubach•

Lakeview• •Bossier City

West Monroe•

Shreveport•

Natchitoches•

•Georgetown

Ferriday•

•Colfax

Paradise•
Alexandria•

Marksville•

•Bunkie

•Ang

DeRidder•

St. Francisville

Ville Platte•

New Roads•

Longville•

Fordoche•

Arnaudville•

Bat

Church Point•

•Breaux
•Scott Bridge

Lake Charles•

Lafayette•

Jennings• Crowley•

St. Martinville•

De

Lake Arthur•

Jeanerette

New Iberia•

Abbeville• Lydia•

P

Intracoastal City•

Franklin•

Bayou

Point au Fer Is

4:49 A.M.

MOON FILTERS THROUGH REEDS, mulberries, and moss—silver as sun-stained water. The egret alights, child angel, among wild blue irises. The alligator, cunning, skims the viscous swamp, opens its jaws, snaps shut. One white wing, blood tinged and torn, rocks, rests, in a small cove.

— *Beverly Matherne*

5:00 A.M.

YOU WANT TO CATCH FISH, you have to be there when they're hungry. You fish the marshes for catfish, speckled trout, and redfish as soon as it's daylight. This Saturday that means having your boat ready to be slung into the bayou by an old crane (one dollar per foot of boat length) at Hopedale down in St. Bernard Parish by 5:00 a.m.

There's a line of vehicles, mostly pickup trucks, with trailered boats behind, waiting their turn at the launch. The darkness somehow makes the humidity worse, and the mosquitoes swarm out of the tall reeds, biting and zinging. Your turn comes, you tie your boat to the dock out of the way of the next boat to be launched, and hurry back to park your truck and empty trailer in the weeds by the road.

Careful to make only a small wake, you idle quietly down Bayou La Loutre past the sleeping houses on the east bank, make the final left turn, and pour on the coal until you intersect the Mississippi River Gulf Outlet. They call it "MR. GO." You make a sweeping left turn around the green, triangular channel marker. A half-mile or so and you turn right into an oil company canal heading into the marsh. Straight as a die, the canal spawns a hundred bayous on either side. Your only guide to fishing success is your instinct.

So you anchor a hundred yards down a side bayou, the marsh grass and little trees all around you, butterflies waving madly and white egrets working the mud banks. Then, all of a sudden, a really strange thing happens. Your boat drops like an elevator and lands on the bottom. Unheard and unseen, a gigantic freighter has slid down MR. GO behind you. Its passing displaces so much water in the confined channels that all the water in your bayou is momentarily sucked out. You're looking at the mud bottom, the crab traps, plastic bags, beer cans, and other trash lying there. You spin around in time to see the huge brown hull disappearing toward the Gulf. As quickly as it drained, the water rises again and you bob to the surface. It's as though it never happened.

– Graham Clarke

5:51 A.M.

ON HIS HANDS AND KNEES, Emile strains to see past the early morning curtain of gray mist in Andrus Cove. The light fog shifts around him in rhythm with the air, thicker here than there, then, shifting again, gives first little visibility and then only a little more. The wintry droplets of wetness settle against his face. But Papa Anatole has taught him that a good hunter makes no extra motions, so he shivers as the dew runs down his cheeks and drips from his chin.

He holds the old man's twenty-gauge shotgun lightly against the ground. He has learned about noise too. The rice field was harvested only a week before, leaving a blanket of stubby stalks. If he moves too fast, the crush of rice stubble will give him away. So he inches forward, crawling slowly and making sure not to get dirt in the end of the barrel.

His heart pounds. In moments, he'll break through the fog and catch sight of them. He hears them moving slowly about; muttering, wakened by the just breaking dawn. The impulsive air again disturbs the fog and there they are.

Emile freezes. There are six, no seven. They feel safe because none of them keeps watch for the others. His forefinger finds the safety button near the trigger guard. He's ready. Moving as slowly as a watched snake, he lies down, eases the gun up to his line of sight, and braces it against his shoulder. He aims. The sight falls upon the closest one's head and he fires.

The sharp blast echoes through the fog, shocking the morning awake, followed immediately by an ocean-wave rush of thousands of Canadian geese thrashing the air. Emile is quickly to his knees and fires again into a bird-blackened sky. Feathers fly as one of the big birds whirls upside down and drops.

Though he has two geese for the gumbo, he stands and aims above the fog for a third shot. But as he aims, he finds that the sun has touched the horizon and torched the sky. Rays of bright orange fan out between gray Gulf-of-Mexico clouds scattered across the indigo heavens. Rising across the brilliantly colored background are a thousand black and white geese, now in row after row of *V* formations, in chorus, calling out their hopes, their fears, their celebration, and their mockery of the hunter below. The gigantic formation turns in unison, swings south, as though they are all controlled by one mind. Who knows, Emile thinks. Maybe they are. He smiles and slowly lowers his gun.

— Edward G. Gauthier

5:59 A.M.

NEW DAWN JUNE LIGHT PRIES ITS FINGERS through the passing storm clouds, pushes its way through the heavy rain as it thunders on the metal roof, demanding we hear its music while leaning on the rails of the porch.

Beards of daddy long legs sit quiet, unmoving, listening, watching, waiting for the light, attached to the shelter of this cedar porch roof, here, on the shore north of Pontchartrain.

The rain pounds, careens into the deep drainage ditches, travels down to the Tchefuncte River. It is rain of perhaps the intensity that Noah knew.

Twelve feet from the drainage ditches there are tiny stacked mounds. No matter how hard you look you won't see the crawdads that inhabit them. Don't bother to think of fetching your *piegnon* or strings; they're too tiny to be after with spear and tie. There is not enough water in the red clay soil to grow them big enough for gumbo pots.

The seconds tick by.

The urge to light is now stronger than the lessening energy of the storm clouds moving east.

Tiny squirrels emerge from the deep brown, gnarled, lovingly protective ark of live oaks that were first breaking the soil and clay with their roots a century ago when the big quake rocked San Francisco.

The stray gray cat leaves its refuge under the house.

The neighbor dogs bark their morning greetings down the muddied, potholed, dirt road from one to the other; Great Dane and Mastiff, to Red Hound, to just plain mixed varieties of whatever.

Light gentles away the thinning clouds; ignores the now distant lightning; is deaf to the hollowed thunder, then bursts into brilliant hot yellow, glowing here, dappling there through live oak leaves, steaming them, whispering *wake up* through the blooming gardenias, sago fronds, dark greens of camellias.

The sky shouts blue, impatient now, splits a light rainbow through the sun-sparkled residual slow soft rain.

Cloying steam rises from the grass, drips off your fingers, while meandering steam tendrils wend their way through the pinewoods.

Scores of the nine hundred acres of herbivores at Global Wildlife, tiny and huge, longhaired and short, ever hungry for visitors, add their music to the post-storm morning symphony.

Logging trucks rumble down the highway that flexes and moans under the heavy weight of overloaded flatbeds longer than the living rooms of most of us.

Redbirds, robins, blue jays, woodpeckers, crows give throat to song.

Daddy long legs stretch, flutter their beards.

The new morning light glistens the myriad greens into silvers and gold; disperses the heavy gardenia scent from blooming bushes with ten-foot spans onto a gentle breeze.

— Remy Benoit

6:40 A.M.

IN MORNING'S FIRST LIGHT, the cypress-timbered huts are dim shapes, shrouded in mist rolling in from Cane River Lake and settling over the plantation's grounds and, beyond, its flat fields and pecan orchards. A door creaks on its iron hinges, and a rush of warmth from the big house escapes as Sherman steps onto the back porch to begin his chores. "Thirty-three degrees is cold for Natchitoches this late in February," he sighs, picturing the countless branches he must pick up before noon, when tourists would start to trickle in. Boxed in a gray corduroy jacket, Sherman stoops to lift the basket, big as a cauldron, to his hip, his hands like paddles in brown leather gardening gloves. In the distance, a wood duck whistles, a mourning dove coos. The only other sound is the "cluck, cluck" of Betty the hen as she rustles nearby through the ragged stalks of the lone banana tree, brown and withered now, save for a single, erect, green shoot at its center.

Sherman turns to survey the day's territory, and he catches his breath: the breaking light touches with gold a vast pink-and-white quilt of fallen blossoms covering every inch of earth. "That early spring shower last night rained petals," Sherman whispers, as he whirls to gaze at the towering Japanese magnolias, still laden with cuplike flowers, magenta-stained on the outside, creamy white on the inside, perfuming the misty air with a delicate, orchidlike fragrance. "A lower heaven," Sherman pronounces, as he spots Betty, now roosting on a branch of a great live oak, fringed with green Resurrection fern. Next to her is a Brown Leghorn rooster. Sherman has named this barnyard pimp Lyle Saxon after the writer who once lived here at Melrose Plantation and wrote all his books about Louisiana in the mud-and-moss Yucca House. "Well, Betty," Sherman says with a wink, "looks like all that strutting Lyle did around here lately was for a reason." Betty clucks, Lyle inches closer, and the sun rises.

— Chance Harvey

7:30 A.M.

THE BACK ROADS BETWEEN CROWLEY AND LAFAYETTE run through farm country. People use these roads to avoid the heavy traffic on Interstate 10 or U.S. Highway 90. This morning, a car traveling toward Lafayette on one of these roads makes a right turn and . . . stops. The driver, a middle-aged man, opens the door, gets out, and leans on the front fender, mesmerized by the scene that has caught his eye.

On the right side of the road, the sun is just high enough to highlight a large saucer of water wrapped around by a levee and, beyond that, another levee-wrapped saucer of water. The scene is repeated—water, levee, water, levee—all the way to a horizon defined by small scrub trees, shrubs, and weeds, their soft grays and greens and tans melding and blending into the not-yet-bright-blue of the sky.

The man's eyes search the scene.

He moves closer.

He smells the air, catching the odors of dust, mud, water, and decaying vegetation.

He feels the heat, the humidity making the air heavy and sticky.

For the length of several heartbeats, Time seems to warp and displace the Now, the Present, in his mind. For just a moment, he wonders: Is this a South Vietnamese rice paddy . . . or a South Louisiana crawfish pond?

— *Erlene Stewart*

8:00 A.M.

THE "DHARMA BUMS" REINCARNATED! Wine spodee-odee and all that jazz. But this is a still life after having taken the road again on our literary *wanderjahr* of the South. Asleep in the car it's "Smokin' Joe" Coté, Lenny, and me. Took the wrong turn out of Awlins Town, Highway #23, the "Belle Chasse" to Nowhere, Louisiana.

No canals, no St. Mark's, no Hotel Flora. But Venice, all right. Venice, Louisiana. There's only the cathedral of the wide morning sky stretching over the Gulf of Mexico. . . .

Parked on road's shoulder we raise our heads from the seats to see a jumble of untended shrimp boats half-submerged and slanted in pearly light, the *Donna Marie,* the *Captain Peter,* the *Night Star.*

Damn. It's eighty-four degrees already. Beer cans that chased last night's Jim Beam are now making tinny floor chimes when I move my feet to rise, one shoulder at a time. Air creeps into our rental car windows scented with marsh salt, close, silky, silty soft. Low cloud cover, and the radio lady's voice switched to "On" drifting moodily. Len mutters, "We're movin' light but doin' dark."

Rubbing eyes, I glance to the page of my journal with roadside signs noted. There's Scoop's Seafood Market, Miss Anne's Lounge, the Party Tavern. That sounds mighty good. There's also the signboard reading "Intrepid Fabrications." It tells us what we already know. Writers need life to imitate art.

The Baptist church sign warns: *"It sure is hot, but hell's hotter."*

— *Lou McKinney*

8:11 A.M.

THE RESIDENT BEAT POET OF NEW ORLEANS is sitting on the stoop of a small green flat on Orleans Street in the French Quarter.

His bloodshot eyes are worshiping the sunrise; his mind is trying to pardon itself from the pool of alcohol it's swimming in; his mouth is dragging on a Newport cigarette all the way to the cotton nub. The sun has not completely settled in the fresh morning sky.

He screams an indictment against American culture. He is tall and Irish, with cheekbone-length blond hair and black artsy/intellectual glasses. He is wearing a tuxedo with finely polished black patent leather shoes. He is wearing a green athletic fleece sweatshirt over his tuxedo top with a bib of his own vomit down the center of the fleece. Green fleece streaked with yellow mucus and dried alcohol.

His hands are black from tar and mud and probably crawling in the gutter. The sun rises above the Catholic church in the east and his eyes become illuminated. They are dime-sized sunbursts — phoenixes, devils. His pupils fluctuate in diameter, incongruently, even in the direct sunlight. He is drunk, and probably high on something else — not life.

He laments the loss of true freedom and curses the displacement of American values and the absurdity of war. He does so in a poem, which he recites in a bubbly fever, stopping after every line to massage his stomach and catch his breath. His ambitions are to conform his work to the existing works of Ginsberg, so he says. His poetry is more Ginsberg than an evolving conformity.

He screams indictments against American culture to cars that pass on the street and tells a tall, slim black woman who struts past him she is f---ing cool. The poet likes black women but he hates black men, so he says. He shows the world — which won't listen to him — his scarred hands: deep gashes on his knuckles. The shadow from the crucifix atop the Catholic church is slashing his face in two.

"I had to beat young black men that were robbing old ladies. That's f---in' humanity," he gasps. Young black men are exploiting the structure of freedom in America, according to the poet.

He recites some more of his (Ginsberg's) poetry. He ends his sple-
netic poem by raising his arms and mock-cocking a twelve-gauge
shotgun and blasting the sun. This black-hearted bard wants to
demolish America; he wants to blow it all away, but New Orleans
is safe. New Orleans is not America, so says the poet.

"This is the f---ing foundation, man," he rants, as he stomps his
foot clumsily on the brick-and-cement sidewalk. "The f---ing foundation." The sidewalk he is stomping on is cracked.

He insists on reciting love poems to lovely couples. He serenades
them with the words as they walk by. The poet is persistent. The
lovers are apprehensive of his drunken conviction, so says the
quickening rhythm of their shoes slapping the concrete.

The lovers are gone. The sun is higher now. It's so bright the poet
can no longer see the Catholic church. It's burning right into his
eyes. He is reciting the words of love to the lovers who cannot hear
him. The words are beautiful. They are T. S. Eliot's.

— Cody Whetstone

9:00 A.M.

A PLUME OF SPOKEN WORDS trails from the mouths of three women walking down an icy mud road. "You know we're nuts to be out here bird watching in weather this cold. In two days it will probably be in the sixties." "Yeah, but we would miss all the good winter birds. Hey, look, look." One points to the top of a leafless hackberry tree. Against the china blue sky, a flock of birds settles on the branches and begins feeding on the small fruit. "Cedar waxwings," one lady murmurs and they all nod in agreement, their binoculars pressing tight against their eyes. They watch the small sleek yellow and brown birds flutter about, a splotch of red on the wings like wax and black-masked crested heads identifying them.

All are so wrapped up in the sighting, none notices an old man has joined their group. "What you looking at?" he says. They all gasp and jump in unison.

Although he doesn't laugh, his shoulders shake in obvious delight. He repeats, "What you see?"

Recovering her composure, one lady answers this common question asked of birders. She identifies the birds as cedar waxwings.

"*Mais oui, cirier,* make a good gumbo, yeah," he says, his eyes watching the women with interest.

All turn horrified faces to him. "You would eat them?"

"Well, sure," he says. "When you hungry, you eat anything."

They continue watching the birds sitting in orderly rows in the hackberry and listen to their barely audible high-pitched "zzzzzz." The man seems to be able to see the birds with his old eyes just about as well as they can with their expensive optics.

One lady's mind drifts to a long time ago when this area of Terrebonne Parish was isolated both by culture and geography, especially in the rare hard cold spells. She imagines the man as a young father, a table full of small mouths to feed, a pot of steaming gumbo perfuming a small room, a gumbo full of tiny bones.

As the women turn to leave, one lady says, "You know, it's illegal to shoot them now."

He nudges her lightly with his elbow. Unsmiling, his eyes twinkle in his wrinkled brown face. "Good eating," he says.

— Patricia Allen

9:21 A.M.

MONDAY MORNINGS ART KENDRICK LOADS UP HIS PIROGUE with the dead birds and paddles out in the bayou. He owns a cockfighting ring in Bogalusa, on the Pearl River, the dividing line between Louisiana and Mississippi. Every Sunday during fighting season the crowds gather for this cultural and family event. Grown men walk around with their fighting cocks stroking and talking to them — six-foot, 300-pound rednecks cradling roosters like babies. Four-inch razor blades are strapped to the cocks' feet and they are thrown in to fight for their lives.

On game day, things get started pretty early. The cooking begins about 6:00 a.m. There's Double D sausage and eggs on the griddle. There's a huge pot of Community Dark Roast brewing. The coffee helps wake up and warm the crowd. The various space heaters throughout the barn are not enough to take the chill out of the huge aircraft hangar. It only truly warms up later in the morning, when over two hundred people crowd the bleachers: young and old, men and women, participants and spectators. The bleachers consist of two-by-twelves cut into rough stairs. There are old, salvaged church pews on one side of the ring. Their location and their cushions make them the good seats. You have to get up pretty early for those. The air is cold, the seats are cold, and it smells like damp wood and dung. The winter air is dry and a wind blows up dust from the dirt floor that lies beneath the large ring in the center of the bleachers and the smaller rings off to the side.

Once the round begins, so does the betting. From one side of the ring a man in overalls and a plaid shirt yells, "I've got twenty dollars on the red bird." This is matched with a shout of "I'll take that twenty dollars on the white bird," from a man with a Skoal ring on his back pocket. Excitement is high. Kids are eating hotdogs and speculating with their friends or parents about who will win.

The ref watches up close and the handlers stand aside. One bird sticks its razor clear through the other bird's neck. The ref yells,

"Handle your birds!" The handlers quickly grab their birds. The handler of the injured bird sticks its whole head in his mouth and sucks the blood from his dying bird's lungs. He spits out the blood and sends the revived cock back out to fight.

Once both birds are injured the excitement of the fight slows and the cocks are moved to a smaller side ring. Those who are invested in the fight follow, those who are not anxiously await the next fight. A smaller side ring is set aside for the dead cocks. These birds, only a while ago caressed by their handlers, are now forgotten trash, tossed aside to be disposed of later. Art once rescued a cock from the death pit that wasn't quite dead; it turned out to be quite the fighter.

Now, the day after, Art is alone, paddling out in the bayou, his pirogue loaded with the dead birds. The alligators look forward to these Monday mornings.

— *Cathy Setzer*

9:27 A.M.

9:27 A.M. SPLAYS OUT LIKE ETERNITY in August-Metairie, Louisiana. The sun-so-far-above drones down slow, blazing its white heat in long low waves that bounce even slower off the patchwork of concrete and asphalt stretching out behind the old Oldsmobile dealership on Veterans. All the colors of new shimmer off the cars like Mardi Gras beads glitter on parade days, but slowed with summertime sun. Dirty blue smoke curls up in paper-thin ribbons, anchored at the ashy-red end of a cigarette and the hand holding it draws back, through the millions of water-molecule seas. The seas hold so close together in the heavy humid now, riding waves of sunlight and absorbing thousands of chemicals in the dirty blue smoke. That hand holding belongs to the boy-becoming-a-carsalesMan, waiting for the morning meeting at 9:30. Catching a smoke, waiting for the morning meeting, becoming a carsalesMan in the suburbs of New Orleans, and *what-a-wonderful-life* he thinks, slowly though, like the long low waves of heat and the curling dirty blue smoke, curling down the nicotine into his lungs with a long low drag. It hits him right away, the dizziness of the deep drag he feels at 9:27 in the morning in August-Metairie, in Louisiana. Waving sideways are sounds of the autobay, rippling millions of water-molecule seas, the dat-dat-dat of the air drill, the thick Cajun accent of a mechanic without the substance of his words filtering through. Cajun tone and tenor ride those waves with their own special style — peaked out with a lulling swampy cadence, and the air drill draws in sharp exclamation points at every unknown-sentence-ending. Ashy-red anchor heats the hand holding, and fingers quick-flick what's left of the cigarette toward all those new colors. Selling summertime in the suburbs of New Orleans in August isn't anything the boy-becoming-a-carsalesMan wants to meet about as the minute hand of the clock overhead points him onward to 9:28 a.m.

— *Joshua Leran Holmes*

9:30 A.M.

A COTTAGE INDUSTRY OF LIFE ON THE WATER appears sparingly on Highway 82: hull welders, custom propellers, dry docks, until the body of water becomes consistent, matures to an open span evident for miles. The last land, just before this, is Intracoastal City, surrounded by fields of sugarcane, rice, and crawfish. Decaying barns and storage buildings punctuate the otherwise occupied expanse. The muddied fields are a dense batter of earth and water, incredulously dark. Billet harvesters reap the cane in unison. A hedge of crane peck and rest in the prolific earth.

Tethers to civilization disappear once the boat enters the marsh. The waterways are marked simply with symbols, colors, and occasional crawfish buoys. The GPS crackles indeterminately; the noise from the engine is ceaseless. The occasional boater waves from an opposite direction. The boat enters and exits a maze of hidden passages until the ranger station at the Fearman Refuge appears, a manmade island occupied by a solitary ranger assigned to manage and patrol the entire marsh. American and Louisiana state flags slouch on a pole.

Brother slows the boat to a crawl and maneuvers to the south end of the ranger station to a pier separating the marsh reserve from the public. Another boat is already tied to the pier; a man with a shrimp net is positioning himself to cast. Brother docks, cuts the engine, and begins the business of tying turkey necks to tent stakes with waterproof nylon twine. He prepares an entire packet of necks, climbs onto the dock, and begins dropping them into the water. Within seconds he tugs the cord of a sunken neck and checks for resistance. He grabs a net from the boat, returns to the line, and begins to reel the cord and the neck onto the dock until a crab appears. He gingerly places the net underneath the crab and gives it a shake until the crab releases. With his right leg he reaches over to the boat, kicks open an industrial-size cooler with the name *L. Bernard* sharpied on the lid, and drops in the first of many blue crab.

Translucent jellyfish caught by previous boaters slick the dock; they slurp into the water with a swipe from Brother's foot.

The lead weights from the shrimper's net give a dull thump against the soaked boards. "Det's sum nice creb," says the man in affected Cajun syncopation, noting the crab fighting inside the cooler. Brother wipes his hands on his trousers and watches the man. "See," says the Cajun, "you give it 'nough slack. Hold de net with de left and open de rest with de right. Now, when you t'row it you'll want to twirl it with your wrist. Imagine you dancing with your girl and she twirls around de floor and her skirt lifts up so you can see underneath." The Cajun follows his own instruction and throws the slack net, which bursts into an uninterrupted circle inches before breaking the surface of the water. Brother smiles, kneels onto the soaking pier, gives a tug to each line for the next blue crab to appear.

— Gabriel Gomez

9:37 A.M.

A YOUNG COUPLE EMERGES FROM PINEY WOODS bounded on one side by a small pond and the other by a wide cow pasture. The pond is still, and the cows shuffle lazily about, heads bent down, lipping for grass. The couple holds hands as they approach a little house with a screened-in porch that stretches its entire length.

An older man stands near the house with a holstered pistol snug to his waist. He waves at the young woman, who waves back. "I was checking the cows," he says. "Saw the car."

The young woman introduces the older man, explaining that he lives up the road a bit, near Bunkie, and watches out for her father's farm while they're in New Orleans. While the men shake hands, an armadillo trundles by, oddly oblivious to the nearby people. The caretaker spots it, lifts the pistol from his waist, clicks the safety, and fires. The sound seems strangely muffled in the quiet morning, as if the thick, wet air dulls the gun's pop, and the armadillo tumbles over without a noise, though it writhes and flails its claws in the air. "Your father around?" asks the caretaker, wandering over to the squirming animal.

"No," she says, "it's just us for the weekend."

He nods, picks the armadillo up by its tail, and smashes it against a tree. It stops wriggling. "Well, tell him hello for me."

"Sure," she says.

The caretaker walks off, carrying the dead armadillo. The body dribbles blood, though not nearly as much as the young man thinks it should.

"What the hell was that?" he asks.

She shrugs. "They're pests," she says.

— Dale Hrebik

9:47 A.M.

THEY DON'T KNOW HER NAME, but they know that some of the people who talk to her get to leave. They know they want to leave, and they hope she can help.

"Teacher! Hey, teacher! Please!"

Her eyes scan the pod. There are no bars at Caddo Correctional Center, only metal doors, rectangular windows, eyes. It's impossibly loud, and she is wondering how such loud voices can come from such small eyes. She hears the desperation in the voices and mistakes it for urgency or boredom or some strange form of flattery. When she is gone, the deputy will hit the intercom button and announce the consequence for yelling.

She counts the number of footlockers outside the door. Four inmates are on suicide watch. Inside, she knows, those inmates are dressed in blue. There is an awkward moment when she realizes that she too is wearing blue and she stops midstep. The voices coming from behind her stop. Perhaps they think she will turn around. She quickly resumes her pace, and the calls continue.

"Teacher! Everything you need to know! Me!"

The interviews, the medical gowns, the eyes have changed her. For her, blue is not the color of a summer sky or a baby blanket. Blue is a bed sheet turned noose, a footlocker beside the phrase *blunt head trauma*, a ten-degree temperature drop. Last week she heard about a woman who tried to kill herself by chugging balled pages of a Gideon's Bible. It seems to her like the punch-line of a bad joke.

Instead of thinking about this, she focuses on the task ahead. She's counting her steps. The deputy beside her reminds her of the time. She's tallying her questions, her steps, the number of times she hears the word "teacher." She's nearing his cell. The intercom clicks on and then announces.

"192476, uh, 93098 . . . you got company!"

They left the rookie manning the station. It's unusual for her to conduct interviews in the pod, but Mr. Timer only got out of the infirmary yesterday.

"He's still not walking so good," the deputy says. "But that Timer is still ticking."

The joke is a bad one since they both know that the one thing that Mr. Timer doesn't have is time. One of the tumors they removed from his liver last week was the size of a small child's fist. Outside of his cell, she bends down to look in through the serving slot. The proximity of his eyes startles her. In the last few weeks the whites of his eyes had faded into a muted yellow. Today that yellow is bright with interruptions of red.

Dried spit sits in the corners of his mouth as he extends a shaking hand through the serving slot toward her. When she shakes it, she feels his raised veins. This is the first time they have ever touched.

She pulls back her hand faster than she means to and watches as he pulls the photos of his family out of his Bible. When his photos are in his hand, he is ready to begin. This is his routine. Neither of them knows that this is the last time they will see each other, but they both have a hunch. When he starts to cry, she forgets her questions and the number of steps. She notices that the voices calling for her attention are gone. Only the eyes remain.

— Sunday Angleton

9:52 A.M.

"THIS IS IT." The old man gestures to his right by tapping the window on the passenger side four times in rapid-fire succession with his middle finger. "Just pull in alongside the van." The window tapping begins again. The Gray Ghost, an ancient Mercury Grand Marquis, aches and groans as it bounces toward the carport, unsuccessfully dodging holes the size of bean pots as it makes its way down a driveway lined with oyster shells. The side panels of the van come into full view, a rolling advertisement for Slick's Photography and Guns ("We'll shoot ya' one way or the other") eye level as the occupants emerge from the Ghost. First the old man hoists himself up and out of the car and then, tentatively, a strapping Illinois farm boy, square-jawed and too tall to be from around here, emerges from the driver's side, the old man's son-in-law, making his first trip to South Louisiana, to Thibodaux, to be exact.

They're going out on the water today, and Slick is the old man's fishing partner in a place where every man has a fishing partner, where fishing partner (or hunting buddy, depending on the season) is actually what men call each other instead of "friends." Today they're headed down to Pointe au Chien, but it's already midmorning and already mid-June and, at this rate, they'll be putting in just as the reds and specks are sinking down low in search of the quiet and the cool.

The car doors shut, one after the other, with a satisfying *thwack.* The guys toss their tackle boxes in the joeboat and head toward Slick's house, a rambling cypress shack with a trailer hidden somewhere beneath it all. A system of walkways crisscrosses the sewage ditch and leads on one end to Slick's photography studio and on the other to the reloading room, where he cleans his guns, sharpens his knives, and spruces up his Civil War reenactment paraphernalia. Massive interlocking vines hold these additions together, anchored by poison ivy plants with leaves as big as the young man's feet. Squeezing by, careful not to brush against anything, the men walk on ahead, beyond the carport, to the edge of the swamp, where heaps of carcasses bake in the sun.

The son-in-law regards it all less out of curiosity than with the wary eye he has developed in his ten years as a patrol officer, walking his beat through some mighty frigid winters, worlds away from a day like today. Hollowed-out crab shells, bleached crawfish heads, translucent shrimp hulls—shellfish mausoleums with little to offer the flies frequenting the gravesites. If it can be eaten, the odds are good that Slick has eaten it first. As a bonus, the smell attracts critters, possums and coons especially, which Slick shoots with his .22 from the swivel rocker in his living room. Straight through the screen door. The irrefutable evidence of Slick's unorthodox technique—sixteen holes in the screen, each the size of a pockmark, the blast pattern consistent with a shot fired from the inside. "That boy's the laziest bastard I ever known," the old man remarks, "but he's a damn good shot for a blind fella."

Just then, the host emerges from the dark recesses.

"Hey, what ya know, B." Slick's movements are quick but they're jerky and oddly off balance, a lot of energy going nowhere fast. His speech is much the same, thickly Cajun with frequent sputters and tics that step on everyone else's toes. Clean-shaven and freshly groomed, his personal hygiene stands in stark contrast to his housekeeping skills. Glasses thick as a two-by-four rest unevenly on his nose, held together at every joint by wads of duct tape.

At the old man's urging, Slick demonstrates his screen-door point-and-shoot technique, complete with firearm retrieved from beneath the La-Z-Boy; then he offers a five-cent tour of the place. The son-in-law moves slowly and cautiously through the maze, ducking beneath light fixtures and doorjambs. They pause only briefly in the Hall of Co-Eds, where framed glossy yearbook photos of lovely undergrads hang askew. Most were taken, Slick explains, during his stint as the official graduation photographer at several local schools. "Don't worry," the old man points out, a glint in his eye, "they're all accounted for." Which, as far as anyone knows, is true.

— *Elizabeth H. Boquet*

10:00 A.M.

As I ENTER THE COOLNESS of St. Paul's Episcopal Church in Abbeville, pulling open the thick, solemn, engraved doors and passing into the sanctuary, a rainbow lights the darkness from window after window of stained glass. Pictures of saints: Augustin, Theodore, Louis, Peter, Joan of Arc, Jesus, and then you—I stop, drawn to your little face. Your curly golden hair surrounds a sweet ethereal countenance, pink-cheeked, a partial smile on your lips as if you know a secret but can't tell. Little Henry Edwards, immortalized and forever young. What is your story?

"Son of Dr. and Mrs. Clarence Edwards," I read below your picture, yet he couldn't save you, Henry; I wonder why. Did it haunt him the rest of his life? There is an angel standing over you, holding your hand—your little fingers grasp back tightly, trustingly. She shields you with wings of pale white, covering you like a silk blanket. Why do you smile? Are you thinking of your mother? Is she still here, somewhere in this town, coming to light a candle each day for you and praying still for God to heal the empty space in her heart where faith no longer lives since you left her? At night when she lies awake, does she still feel your soft skin and smell your hair and hear your voice saying, "Momma?" She must come here to sit and look at you on days when she can no longer bear the stillness of her house, of her thoughts, of being alone. You hold a cross against your heart. Are you still smiling, Henry?

I have a son, Henry. He is only a year old and like you he has hair like ripe corn silk and serious eyes of brown that hold mysteries, too, and sometimes I sneak into his room at night and lay my hand on his back, checking to make sure he's breathing. (I have done this since my husband made me put him in that baby bed so far away from me.) I wake up some nights, heart pounding, and listen to the dog snoring beside my bed and the soft, steady breath of my husband and then it comes—the sweat and my heart against my chest and I wonder about him and hesitantly get up. The walk to his bedroom is long and fearful and until I put my hand there on the back of his T-shirt and feel it, the rhythmic up and down staccato beat of his heart, there is a tingle in my chest that almost chokes me. I think you must be shaking your head and laughing at me now, Henry. But I wonder if your mother ever did the same.

— Jerre Borland

10:10 A.M.

OCTOBER MORNINGS ARE THE BEST TIME OF THE DAY of the best month in South Louisiana. The day's heat hasn't set in yet, the sky is blue, and breeze sweeps the air. All Saints' Day is coming up next weekend. Families have come to the cemetery to take care of the graves of their dead.

An old lady moves with a walker through the middle of the cemetery. She is with her granddaughter and her granddaughter's husband, and they are looking for the graves of her mother and father. She used to know exactly where they are. . . .

They had come down this morning from Baton Rouge on La. 1. They passed sugarcane fields and chemical plants. Many of the houses they passed had blue Virgins in the yard. And they had come through the place of her birth. Although the house no longer stands there at Grand Bayou, she recognized the place by the old mossy oak tree, which remains as a grave marker of sorts. The marker had directed them to the Paincourtville cemetery, and now she had to find . . . aaah, here they are . . . the graves of Adia Landry and Joseph Albarado.

Her granddaughter opens the lawn chair for her, and she sits in the shade and watches as the younger woman and her husband begin scrubbing the elevated graves in preparation for whitewashing.

Several others at the same task stop by during the morning. A few recognize the old lady; others introduce themselves and ask whom she is related to and how. Her granddaughter listens to all the stories about the families and about the old days—about the men tracking and killing the alligator that had bitten Parrain Petit's leg in 1935 until he gouged out the alligator's eye with the spur on his boots used to climb trees to collect moss for mattresses; of the time every spring when the waters came and the families would put their furniture as high as they could and leave in a flatboat to "where the water ended"; about how as a girl Nolda and her girl-friend Icy would fix a big bowl of sweet potatoes, raw with salt, pepper, and vinegar, and climb up to the roof to eat them. Laughs and memories connect the pieces, and there is a connected peace.

The sun rises higher, the graves are painted, and they decide that the job is good enough for another year. They return to the car, and the lady directs them to a service station/restaurant where she insists on buying fried shrimp po' boys. She puts her hand on top of her granddaughter's. She is not sure that she will be here next year, but her anxiety is gone: she knows in her bones that the graves will be tended.

— *Mike and Stacy O'Rourke*

10:30 A.M.

A FLOCK OF CANVASBACK DUCKS, pale gray and white with ruby-red eyes, cuts through the crisp October air in a *V* shape, outpacing the SUVs and pickup trucks crawling across the Mississippi River Bridge into Vidalia. Beneath them, the flat and steady track of Highway 84 is littered on either side with endless strip malls. On the outskirts of nearby Ferriday stands a lone place of worship, a brown, barnlike building. The Church of God marquee on wheels sits at the edge of the road, its blue plastic letters proclaiming, "Walmart is not the only saving place."

At Ferriday, the highway turns west. Within a few miles, a vast cotton field appears, stretching like a giant Monopoly board to the far horizon. An oblong office building occupies Park Place; in the distance, past Luxury Tax and Short Line Railroad, sits a row of tiny cabins with red tin roofs. All 1,800 acres are rich in the soil of easy growth, nourished by repeated flooding of river bottoms. Some fifty yards behind the office looms the computerized public gin, the cream tin structure labeled "Tanner & Co." in red, four-foot-high letters. It produces 800 to 1,000 bales a day.

Lynette Tanner sits behind her desk in the office and runs her hands through her shoulder-length auburn hair, taking a last look at ag updates, scanning the computer screen for worldwide cotton prices. She logs off and phones the gin.

Dorothy Smith, fifty-five, the same age as Lynette, releases the joystick that operates the suction pipe. She cuts the power, silencing the hum of the heavy-gauge metal cylinder. Dorothy exits the glass booth, runs down the stairs, and walks past the trailer she has just whisked clean of cotton. "Who we got this time?" she asks, slipping into the passenger seat. "Some students from LSU," Lynette says, grinning, as she wheels her Volvo away from the gin. "We've got exactly ten minutes to change."

Turning left onto Highway 84, the car sails past the blanket of snow. At this moment, the sun dries the last drop of dew from the leaves of the plants, and, on cue, the red harvest machines begin to rumble through the field. Nearby stand the yellow, high-walled module builders that pack the picked cotton into large blocks for ginning. The men raking spilled cotton off the ground or tagging various farmers' cotton have temporarily escaped from the Concordia Parish Correctional Facility. In the work release program, they get minimum wage, workman's compensation, and days of freedom.

Nearly two hundred years into the past, Lynette, mistress of Frogmore Plantation, emerges from the two-story, columned big house wearing a long, black cotton dress trimmed in white eyelet with pantalettes and full petticoat, her hair upswept in a pearl clasp. She walks the short distance to the mid-1800s plantation church and greets her tour group.

In a nearby slave cabin, Dorothy, whose ancestors were slaves at Frogmore, entertains her tourists with cooking methods circa 1850. Dressed in an ankle-length, gray cotton muslin shift and white apron, Dorothy places a "hoecake" — a cornmeal pancake — on the blade of a hoe and warms it over the fire. Suddenly, a recording begins to play, filling the cypress-timbered shack with song: *The gospel train's a-comin'. Get on board, little chillun. The gospel train's a comin'.* "Of course," Dorothy begins, "the train they are referring to was the Underground Railroad. . . ."

— *Chance Harvey*

10:35 A.M.

TRICIA'S MOTHER, CATHERINE, shouted, "Roll up the windows and get down on the floorboard. Lock the doors and get down, now! Hurry!" It was a hot and sunny day in May of 1968. Too hot, even at 10:30 in the morning, to have all the windows rolled up in the car, for sure. Tricia could feel the sweat beading up on her face and in her hair. There was sandy grit underneath her hands and knees from the dirty black rubber floor mats of her parents' Ford Fairlane station wagon.

One of the three Klansmen was tapping on the passenger window with his knuckle and making a rolling gesture with his forefinger and hand in a vain attempt to get Catherine to roll the window down so he could give her a piece of paper with big black lettering—the page overflowing with Klan propaganda. Tricia couldn't make out much of what they were saying, but she understood the hate in their tone and the word "nigger."

Maybe those men thought Tricia's father was a "nigger" too. After all, Len Doughty had thought so. His first words to her at school had not been "hello" or "may I carry your books?" Instead, he'd said, "Your father is as black as a nigger." The statement was very matter of fact, like it was the gospel, and he'd said it right in front of the whole class. Then, Len smiled at her as the class snickered. Tricia missed the joke, somehow.

"My father is part Choctaw Indian and just got back from Saudi Arabia, I'll have you know!" was her curt retort. She was *not* going to let Len or any of her classmates make her ashamed of her father's golden skin.

Tricia hated living in Dubach. Hate. There was not as much of it here as there was in the large cities or as much of it as she watched on television at night but hate did exist here. Now, hate was standing right outside their car dressed in white flowing robes and pointy hoods.

Tricia's mother forgot the car was already running so the motor made a grinding noise when she turned the key. "S---," she said. "Kids, no matter what, don't open the doors." Their mother backed the car onto Main Street, leaving the Klansmen still standing in the parking space. All Tricia could see was their eyes.

"One of them sounded just like Billy Joe Clary," Catherine would say to Tricia's father that night after they thought the kids were asleep. "I know that was him because I recognized his voice."

"Hmmm," Tricia thought silently to herself. Hate, it seems, owns the gas station and the town's diner, too.

— Patricia Baker

10:43 A.M.

HARRY ANSWERS THE BULLHORN of the Red Cross food truck the way a boy answers the spit of a nun's whistle calling him in from recess. He appears at his door and with a squint surveys North Villere Street as if to assure himself he has heard correctly. Gingerly he picks his way down the cement steps of the turquoise shotgun house. The steps are piled high with black plastic bags brimming with his worldly goods. They are arranged there, barricade style.

His Shadow doesn't bother with the wrought-iron handrail. He leaps nimbly over the same bags. Once landed, he too looks up and then down the same street as if choosing between two colorful posies to carry to his girl, then smoothes the lapels of his orange brocade jacket.

The scents of stale urine and greasy food are trapped among the layers of sweaters and shirts Harry wears to ward off the unseasonable January cold. His thinning gray hair, the part not covered by his cap, sports curled balls of old lint. His lone remaining tooth, yellowed, peeks out only when he smiles.

His Shadow sets off east toward the streetcar that will fetch him uptown, to where the dancing is. A smile breaks across his face echoing the tune his shoe heels strike out as they clatter against the pavement. He hums to the rhythm of his walk. He salutes his auntie, Momma Rose, who fans herself, perched on her front porch in a faded blue rocker. He treats her to a wolf whistle. She shouts back, "Ya gwon, na, Harry. Y'all couldn'a handle what I got ta give, baby." Her laugh trails him down the street arched over with fragrant oak boughs.

Harry steps gingerly over a piece of yellow siding ripped from a house around the corner. The storm blew it there and city workers have not hauled it away. He sidesteps it from habit, though once its brightness stuck out against all the gray debris. He turns his gaze to the crooked sidewalk, minding his step lest he break another bone.

His Shadow is headed to the arms of his crescent mistress. She is a mahogany woman who enflames him simply by wrapping him in the warmth of her jasmine-scented arms. Just as often, though, she flings his affections windward and cackles at his feeble attempts to desert her.

And now, Harry's old mistress is on her knees vomiting waste of all sorts onto the streets. Harry stands by, close. The arthritis that has bent him nearly in two prevents him from hauling his mistress to her feet by himself. Instead, he whispers words of soft encouragement that only she can hear.

"Come on, my darlin'. Stand, na. We gots to get you cleaned up so we's can go dancin'. It's near Carnival time."

Harry turns slowly away from the truck, his food bags slung over his arm, and picks his way back again toward the cluttered front steps. He chuckles quietly as he goes. His Shadow follows, a silent smile on his face, in slow step with Harry.

— *Marianne Mansfield*

10:55 A.M.

AFTER A SPRING FLOOD IN NEW ORLEANS, it is quiet and the air is still, charged with the mineral essence of damp earth, decaying wood, and lingering ozone. After the hard rains, the banana trees shine like exotic green fan blades, their ridges still incandescent with moonglow.

It is Sunday morning, the day after the flood, and the French Quarter is empty. No merchants, no tourists, no Lucky Dog man, no breakdancers, no cars. The water has subsided, but the fear and dread have not. There is no one yelling, no Dixieland streaming out of dark bars, no cloppity-clop of horses pulling carriages. Jackson Square seems totally abandoned, then, straight through the turbid atmosphere comes a woman's voice. It is a strong, steady voice, singing "Bye Bye Blues."

The brown-haired woman, who can't be more than twenty-five, if she is that, wears a long skirt and holds a megaphone. She continues singing through it: "Sun is shining, no more pining. . . ." The melody is heartbreaking; she knows this. Slowly, people appear, mopping up sidewalks, removing wet rugs, and quietly exchanging stories.

"Don't sigh, don't cry," she sings to them. "Bye bye blues."

— *Diane Elayne Dees*

11:05 A.M.

"Betcha never heard a' Lydia."

"Can't say I have, 'cause I ain't."

"That's 'cause it ain't even a wide spot in the road. The road jes' barrels on through without even a speed limit sign."

"So — where'n hell is it?"

"On Weeks Island Road, south of State 90. And don't go tellin' me you never heard a' Weeks Island, neither."

"Can't say I have, 'cause I ain't."

"Ain't you never been outta the city limits a' Monroe, boy? You don't know nothin'."

"Whyn't you quit your braggin' and tell about Linda?"

"Lydia, I said."

"Whatever."

"No speed limit signs, no cops, no fire station, no school, not even a Baptist church, can you 'magine that? *In Lou'siana?* Nothin' but sugarcane fields as far as you can see, which ain't far 'cause the cane's about twelve foot high. All green an' waving in the afternoon breeze, can't see more than a foot through it 'cause it's so thick."

"That's it? A road, an' cane fields?"

"Didn' say it was, did I? I ain't got to the good part yet. Now listen heah. They's a few houses with them tin roofs, kids' toys an' crappy cars out front, an' a fillin' station with a store inside. They sells some right good cracklin's in a bag, local made stuff an' good an' fresh. Bag a' cracklin's an' a couple a' cold Dixies, that's the way to spend a summer afternoon."

"That's the good part? Fried pork hide an' beer? I can get that right here at this bar. Alls I gotta do is call Mikey over."

"No, that ain't the good part, genius. Here's the good part. The gal behind the counter workin' the cash register, she a mulatto, ya know? What we useta call a briquette in N'Awlins. But she is drop dead beautiful. Mos' beautiful gal I ever seen. Beautiful black hair, straight and down on her shoulders. Beautiful eyes, kinda green, little nose, lips like all them movie stars got now, a figure your brain wasn't even made to imagine, and wearing tight pink shorts an' an Army T-shirt. Lord, she was beautiful. I mean, beautiful! Bare feet, too. Beautiful bare feet with teeny little toes an' the nails painted pink like her shorts."

"So, she'd have been beautiful, then?"

"'Tweren't jes' that. I seen all kindsa gorgeous females, but this'n were different. This'n actually *looked* at me. Ain't no woman looked at me in th'eyes since the fire. She done looked at me like I was a real human bean, not some freak. She smiled real nice, ast me how wuz I feelin', ain't it hot out, what nice big shoulders I got. Made me feel like a *man* fer the first time since Claudelle th'owed me out. I hadda say g'bye right quick 'fore she seed the tears in m'eyes."

"Damn. This calls for two more. Hey, Mikey!"

— Graham Clarke

11:15 A.M.

THE OLD PHOTOGRAPH I AM HOLDING shows me, about three years old, and an old black man, Nathan. He is holding my hand and my other hand is holding a toy pistol he has carved for me from a block of cypress. The photo was taken in 1926, about quarter past eleven in the morning. Nathan worked for my father, manager of a Gulf Oil filling station in New Iberia. One of my earliest memories is the day Nathan took me on my first fishing trip—I was about five or six years old.

Early that morning I went down to the Gulf station with my father and then walked across Main Street for breakfast at the Frederick Hotel. Then Nathan and I set off walking down Main Street to Brooks' Stable, located next door to LeBlanc & Broussard Ford Company. My father had gotten permission from Mr. Saul Brooks to dig for worms in the stable. I can still smell the rich, pungent odor of the stable where Mr. Brooks kept his inventory of new and used mules for sale. We quickly filled our bait can and made our way around the corner of Weeks Street to the bank of Bayou Teche.

Nathan brought two cane poles and showed me how to load the hook with squirming, slimy worms. I was squeamish about it but, being the big man that I was, I didn't let on and followed his lead. After overcoming that obstacle, it was lines in the water to wait for the big one.

Well, I wish I had a good fish story to tell, but it was not to be. After about an hour or so we had hooked one small perch, which we threw back. We decided to give the rest of the worms to the fish and go home. I learned a lot about fishing that day, like they don't always bite—but it was a great adventure for me. I think Nathan had a good time, too.

—R. C. Sealy

11:24 A.M.

SO WE GO OUT TO THE CAFÉ on a windy, steamy day that's more like pensacola beach than new orleans, and there is anne, reading a book called *the mind of god,* and robin who recognizes somebody passing on the street just from her back, and i say, "what's new?" and anne says, "there is a nine-year-old girl who just raised money to buy bullet-proof vests for k-9 police dogs," and laura says that she actually saw the news where some crazy felon ran from the police and hid under a house and shot a police dog, which was terrible and that's probably what the nine-year-old girl thought, and i just had my eighth cup of coffee and i have no idea what my column this week is going to be all about, so i say, "i'm going to raise money to buy protective gear for cockroaches" (which in louisiana are big and sentient like little crunchy dogs), and anne says, "little boxes," and i say, "yeah, little boxes where only their heads and legs stick out and there is a little warning light and a taped voice that says just as you're about to step on them: 'agrrhr rrr kstn,'" and laura points out that the calliope on the river is playing "that's amore," and we discuss post-modern literature for some reason, with robin pointing out that *the mind of god,* presently lying next to my coffee cup, has an introduction to an introduction, and i describe (in a few dozen words) nabokov's *pale fire,* which as everyone knows is a crime novel disguised as an academic gloss on a long and bad poem, and anne says, "don't forget compassion," apropos of the kind child who cares about k-9 safety, and i say, "no, of course not," because if column-writing is about anything it's about high moral standards and lessons about life, even the life of cockroaches (i am a jain) and then we discuss the art show by sex workers which has just opened in new orleans, and i think that it's the same show i saw in portland last year, which showed the work of about three hundred sex workers, and then we say goodbye for now to anne and robin, and oh, i forgot, she said that there was a real-estate convention in town and five realtors told her that i was great, and last week there were dentists all over and everybody was smiling, now that's the human world, happily we don't need bullet-proof vests here, and i feel compassion, yes i do, and i forgot about this poem laura and i made up walking down the street to the café that goes partly, "too young to shave/in a world of clueless tourists," which i wrote down with some more lines in anne's notebook for her to make a little book out of, and i'm sure there are a lot of other things i forgot or that i can't tell.

— *Andrei Codrescu*

11:57 A.M.

IT IS A JEALOUS SUMMER HEAT. The hot air has arms and legs. The temperature snatches at one's entire being. It forces the young girl to give up on her windblown hair. Her skirt teases sticky legs from the sun's drenching wet fingers. She drowsily walks along the bright day. It is quiet. There are no birds singing. The sun has chased them from the sky to wait out the evil high noon. The grass is dead from lack of rain. The soil is dry like an old woman's skin. She continues to slowly drag along and stops in front of a small shacklike house. It hardly seems to coincide with the loving description of a home. The fact that it is even fit, or was ever fit, to shelter humans puzzles the girl. The outside walls are constructed from some type of mud mixture. The unforgiving sun has bleached them beyond white, almost transparent. She runs her finger down the front wall. Her fingers trail after every bump and nick. She looks up. The roof is poorly built out of some type of wooden stilts and straw. She steps across a wooden beam, guessing it to be the door frame, and goes inside. The quiet outside is nothing compared to the inside of the shack. The girl shuts her eyes momentarily. Perhaps she is thinking of past lives sitting at the hearth. The fireplace is nothing more than a gaping whole and crumbly crimson bricks. The floor is parched dirt. She kicks a few rocks and pebbles as she walks around. She is told slaves lived here. She is told slaves ate here. She is told slaves gave birth here. The heat is still greedy. Her skirt continues to stick to her damp ankles. Even so, the girl shivers and walks back out into the sun.

— *Sarah Elisabeth Roussel*

HIGH NOON

DOWN. SET. GEAUX.

Gators in town, rightly waving their index fingers, wanting to know what we've got.

So, I tell them.

I've got five pints of Jim Beam strapped to my back and thighs. I've been up since Thursday. Today is Saturday. Today is game day. This is Death Valley.

Ninety-six degrees in the oaken shade. This ain't Mardi Gras, no, but it feels like it.

I know everybody here. The andouille man, the half-assers, the gumbo folks that sit beneath the tree-fan, but they don't know me. Still, today I wear the right colors so they lob me icy beers like ten-yard slants. Tomorrow we may all crawl back into the concrete, sure, but *today*, they say, *what's ours is* all *of ours*.

So, I catch them. Crack them open. I pass one over to Dough, my buddy with the titanic heart. He's a Baton Rouge guy who works like a serf at Brew-Bacher's Restaurant, smuggling hot wings and po' boys back to our place whenever possible, feeding his wages into video poker. He requested this day off seven months ago. We all did. This is game day, by God, this is prime-time against number one, and we are in this together.

Dough's excited.

He shaved his head last night at 6:00 a.m.

He stood atop our living room table as he did this, the stereo bumping, a few blond-headed maybes watching him from our couch with crossed legs. *This is good mojo,* he told them, *this is what it takes to win!,* and his hair fell like a blasted duck's feathers.

Then, all together, us and the girls, we saw the dawn.

But now my friend is crashing. It's understandable. It's high noon under hot sun.

Still, *This type of love is a marathon!* I tell him, and slap my buddy hard on the head. He agrees, opens his eyes with his fingers, and I rub the stubble on his skull for good luck. *Look at all this bait,* I tell him. *Wouldn't you love to send them packing? Wouldn't it sing to pull off a miracle?*

I'm on it, Dough says, and I believe him.

Because Baton Rouge is ours.

This is the place of our birth. It is cracked tar and jungle hot all the time. It is unmowed medians and copious billboards, spent chewing gum boiling up on our sidewalks. This is the unshaven neck of the Mississippi River, the bulbous brain of Cancer Alley, and we have bullet holes, like sores, on our capitol building.

So, we take a lot of s---.

But, we also have *this.* We have right now and today, these few simple acres of purple and gold, and, therefore, we allow no blasphemous tread. In *this* minute, we roam the stadium grounds like the Bengals we adore. We pass bottles and palm smokes. We wait for evening to pull in like a train.

We are not alone.

It's only noon now, sure, it's still early, but it *will* become night in Death Valley.

It *will* become the heart of our state.

So, forgive us our frenzy. Forgive us our shouts.

It's hot here. We may not win.

But we keep cool by the breath of our chorus.

— M. O. Walsh

12:04 P.M.

THE SCREEN DOOR IS PAINTED GREEN and squeaks. Crawfish on newsprint, boiled red with pop-eyes burning black from cayenne, and cold Jax beer in brown bottles, with Satchmo rupturing an old brown radio in the back room. Hear the bottle tops' metallic burp seconds before fizz collides with Tabasco on an old man's tongue. No neighborhood gossip, only the game in black and white from a beery corner, the bat's crack outdone by shells splitting, piled high as Grandma's worries.

No interest in slot machines — that handful of change could buy another beer — but baseball, where plates are marked clearly, measured inch by yard, and success comes almost by instinct, an eye on the ball and a glove in the air. Vicariously he spits tobacco juice from the bulge in his cheek, pulls his cap down, and waits for fate to look him in the eye. Now time for the last swallow of lager and out again into the cancer-god sun to read gas meters, drive home in the black bubble-hooded Pontiac to make another child or two, and wake up to biscuits, molasses, and grits, with just enough time on Earth to teach his grandchildren their bedtime prayers.

In the tropical wetness of a New Orleans summer, where the *Natchez* blows its horn over the crescent river, and the neighborhood edging the Quarter has buried the old-timers in St. Louis Cemetery, we drive away, high noon, eyed by hostile natives sitting on stoops, high on crack. I want to call out to them as they diminish in the mirror:

My grandfather was born here and hung his hopes on a barstool long before you sat your despair on that curb and shot up one more time behind the old shed on Frenchmen. My grandpa leaned on that bar, left a dollar for the barman, and walked out pocketing pennies, turning the corner where bougainvilleas pour pink suds over a wooden fence and trolleys clang down a street saturated with mildew and magnolias.

— Donna Pucciani

12:17 P.M.

THE DOZEN OR SO PATRONS sitting on benches and rocking chairs on The Front Porch in Roseland look toward the door as the bells jingle and it opens. The smell of fried food slowly drifts outside as a young man holds the door open for his very pregnant wife and little boy.

"They must be Catholic," an old man says to his wife.

A chorus of stomachs rumbles as the famished churchgoers all think about their favorite foods on the buffet spread. Some of the families from the Methodist church scrambled out of their pews as soon as the organ began the closing hymn. Their attempts to beat the rush and be the first to fill their plates up with seafood gumbo, chicken and dumplings, fried fish and chicken, buttery biscuits, cornbread, yellow squash, fried okra, black-eyed peas and rice, and green beans miserably failed. They hope there will still be plenty of dessert left when they finally get a table.

Two elderly women, both wearing brightly colored pantsuits, make their way up the steps of The Front Porch. "Did you put our name in the pot?" Ruthie asks her friend who is already waiting.

"I sure did. It looks like a long wait today," Mildred says. "But I was ahead of most of these people," she adds, half-whispering. Mildred picks up her purse, which was saving the spot next to her. She scoots over on the bench and Ruthie and Norma sit down next to her.

"Thank goodness," Norma replies, looking around at the eighteen or twenty people now sitting on benches and rocking chairs and standing up where they can find a place. "At least the weather is nice," she says of the mid-sixty-degree January day. "It just gets so miserable in the summer, it's almost not worth the wait."

"I really like Brother Bruce, but his sermons are longer than Brother Travis's," Mildred says of the new Methodist pastor.

Several more cars arrive and must park across the street because the small gravel lot in front of the restaurant is full.

"Well the Catholics always get here first, but at least we beat the Baptists," Ruthie says.

— *Kathlyn Kastner*

12:30 P.M.

PALO ALTO PLANTATION IS NOT ON THE TOURIST MAPS. Never was. We circle back on La. 1 along Bayou Lafourche well off the River Road drawn by a back road lined with solid live oaks like aged, arthritic sentinels leading the way past the modest white main house into a world long gone yet lingering as if slave hands had just wandered off on a lunch break, their damp sweat hanging in the stifling noon heat, more cloying in its way than vetiver, the sachets of native swamp-grass roots tied with ribbon and sold in French Quarter boutiques.

Cypress weatherboard cabins of the field hands — one slightly larger denotes an overseer — molder among spider webs, never painted, their grays and browns still vibrant in filtered sunlight. Near a large wooden shed a new John Deere tractor and several skeletal cane trailers to keep it company face out over miles of deep green cane fields waving like swamp grass; they are waiting for grinding season still months away.

Breaking the silence a saddled horse neighs impatiently beside the road, its rider off to who knows where; the sweaty odor is still there, and it occurs to me that the last time we shopped for vetiver sachets in New Orleans, they were imported from Indonesia.

— *Mary Gehman*

12:34 P.M.

IF THERE'S SOMETHING TOURISTS FIND UNPLEASANT about Jackson Square on a blistering early afternoon in May it's lost on this crowd, bustling and scurrying around horse-drawn carriages, street vendors, panhandlers, gypsies, tramps, and thieves. In the middle of a small throng of denizens shielding their eyes is a man, quite literally statuesque, standing as motionless as his surroundings upon a small box, painted head to toe in sparkling gold. Rays of sunlight reflect off of him in an infinite number of directions, bright and strong as if being shot straight through him.

A loud, guilty click pounds across this quiet meniscus of immobility. As if the city's very air hears it, a wispy thread of cumulus drifts in front of the sun, just partially eclipsing it. If the taming of the sun is to be any refuge for this crowd, they'll never know. Before they can unearth themselves from their ice, an old white man with a yellowish beard in shoes with six-inch-thick soles, dressed in a red, white, and blue striped suit complete with a matching Uncle Sam hat as high as the bottoms of his shoes, cuts across the street pointing at an unsuspecting photographer with camera trained at the golden man.

"Give that man a dollar!" Uncle Sam screams as he nears the photographer; life resumes around them and heads turn toward the commotion. In the hand that isn't pointing at the man with the camera, liquor spills out of a brown paper bag, leaving a trail across Decatur that if lit on fire couldn't burn Uncle Sam up more than he already is.

"You want to take a picture? Go right up to him and give him a dollar. Don't shoot from a block away!" Sam's finger is pointed right in the photographer's face now, like it is in the posters, in a moment of true surrealism. The finger turns into an empty palm, face up and expectant. "A dollar."

The photographer reaches into his pocket and pulls out a fold of bills. He peels one off and pays Uncle Sam the tax. Sam walks back toward the golden man; his bottle is empty enough now that it's not dripping along the street. Once there, he lets the dollar fall into the golden man's collection. Uncle Sam turns back to the photographer with a scowl of defensive posture, chucks his paper bag into a near-by trashcan, refusing to tarnish his French Quarter with even the prospect of litter.

— Michael Gemme

12:42 P.M.

WHILE HE WAITS FOR A SANDWICH, a policeman is talking about meter maids to an older woman in white, with a German accent, working behind the counter of Croissant d'Or in the French Quarter. "Meter Nazis," he says, "I can't stand 'em either. No, they're not like police officers. They don't carry guns and don't have the power to arrest. They're disgusting. Every one of them weighs about 600 pounds. A few years ago, one is putting a ticket on a police car right in front of the station. An officer comes out, tells her it's a police car, and she keeps writing the ticket. They get into an argument, and she stabs him in the neck with her pen, and he pepper-sprays her. And he gets suspended. Why? Because he was obstructing her from doing her job. What I don't understand is how they're all 300 pounds. All they do is walk around all day long, every day, and sweat, and you'd think they'd lose weight. But they are all 300 pounds. I can't figure that out."

— Richard Louth

1:06 P.M.

ELVIRE WHISPERS, *"POUR L'AMOUR DU DIEU,"* for her ears only. She has been itching to get out into the garden all day. Feather beds had needed flattening by a broken broomstick, chickens had needed feeding, and her own solitary lunch of fresh mustard greens and rice had needed cooking.

But now as the soft spring afternoon beckons, she takes her faded sunbonnet from its hook near the kitchen door. She tucks slit oval earlobes into its folds and ties a loose bow below her wrinkled chin.

Past the dining room table she walks, shoulders hunched. She glances at but does not really see the framed green-and-gray ranks of doughboys behind mustached close-ups of Allied generals of World War I. Padding through the living room, she straightens a ladder-back chair against the beaded board wall where Felicien's piercing blue eyes peer out from a somber face. She calculates again the number of years ago he made her a widow.

An ancient screen door creaks shut behind her as she stands still for a moment on the porch to let her eyes adjust to the sunlight. When her glance falls on the porch-side cistern, Elvire notices for the hundredth time cold rainwater oozing from the faucet onto a green velvet mat of lichen atop a cube of oyster shells naturally cemented together.

She grabs her hoe and breathes in the smell of wisteria vine that has captured the hackberry tree in the corner of the garden, and sniffs gardenias' dizzying sweetness. A whisper of a smile creases her weathered face.

— Claire Domangue Joller

1:29 P.M.

I AM STANDING IN A SUNNY, GRASSY FIELD with Wade Theriot, the *traiteur*,* on his farm less than a mile from the tiny village of Bayou Portage, which lies by the western levee of the Atchafalaya Swamp. Wade treats for any and all complaints and reports decades of successful treatments, "but it's God who does the healings," he insists.

T'Rouge, the glossy orange and black rooster I've just brought Wade, is adjusting to his new surroundings. He steps cautiously around the periphery of a few free-range white chickens. (Wade recently lost a rooster to a chicken hawk and needed another.) I glance at my watch. It's 1:29. I have a headache, and it's still early. There's time for a treatment. Wade agrees to this, and I remove my visor cap so he can place his hand firmly on the crown of my head.

As Wade prays softly in French, I feel heat from his hand as the chickens cluck, scratching and pecking. Then Wade begins to make the sign of the cross repeatedly down the front of my body, without touching my T-shirt or jeans. As he bends his knees to lower himself, he continues to mutter French prayers. When he's reached my dusty boots, he straightens and walks around me to repeat the treatment down my back, still without touching me.

Barely a minute passes before he finishes. We watch T'Rouge as he joins the hens and begins to scratch and peck with them. You don't thank a *traiteur* — thanking is believed to negate a treatment — and I don't as we walk slowly through the field, past his sheep at the trough, and on through the wooden swing gate to the path away from the barnyard. As we pass his old cypress farmhouse, headed toward my pickup, I realize my headache is gone. I smile, wave, and drive away back toward Leonville and my own farm along Bayou Teche.

*A Cajun faith healer or "treater."

— *Karen Yochim*

1:33 P.M.

EASTER SUNDAY 2003. The planet in turmoil. A fast-food emporium on Canal Street in New Orleans. The line six deep. As it moves ever so slowly a guy who is obviously a European, dressed casually as if he were off to a hike as opposed to melting in Dixie, stands incredulous at the ballet of American culture unfolding before him. Every few seconds, he turns with pleading eyes to commiserate with his fellow travelers telepathically, or just to make sure this is actually happening or had he lost his mind?

Behind the counter seven employees hover in a state that resembles mannequins trapped in Jell-O. Everyone in the line has seen this ritual many times but our European friend seems at a loss as to what it is he can do. He just wants it to work. Most people are acquainted with the express line in modern society. This is the Zen line.

"Wheah ya from?" asks the woman waiting in line ahead of him. "My name is Chawlene."

His name is Dieter and he is from Germany. He is on his way to the Lil' Cajun Swamp Tour; the shuttle is about to pick him up at the Marriott around the corner. Chawlene asks rambling friendly questions.

"I work at the D-Day Museum. Ya seen it yet?"

Dieter shakes his head.

Chawlene asks him if he has any favorite local musical groups.

Dieter answers in short jabs of English. It's like Goethe reading *A Confederacy of Dunces* with tweezers. He says, "The New Leviathan Oriental Fox Trot Band."

"Neva hoid a dat one, honey. But I'm shuyah dey good."

Chawlene's order arrives. She departs.

"Have a good time."

"Thank you," says Dieter, who by now is mesmerized by the mercantile tableau in front of him. The pace of service moves at cruise control at best. With the parking brake on.

Dieter arrives at the counter.

The cashier, Kendra, asks if he would like to try "the double combo number five with large fries."

"One five-piece chicken nuggets," says Dieter. He pays, steps aside to wait.

The nuggets are already cooked. They are three feet away at best, visible to all. The other employees continue the fine art of animated nonchalance. This is performance art, perhaps "A Forest of Mimes."

Kendra takes the next order. Dieter stands at the right of the next customer, quiet as a painting at the Louvre. He is a perfect example of placidity at war with itself. Whenever his eyes meet those of another would-be diner, his gaze silently pleads for some explanation of this surrealism.

Still, no one moves to his chicken. At some point during the construction of the next order it occurs to Kendra that perhaps she could fill Dieter's order and the next at the same time. She places his five nuggets into a cardboard pouch, puts the pouch in a bag.

Does she then give them to him? She does no such thing. She puts them on the counter approximately one foot from him.

Does he grab his order? He does no such thing. He does not betray hope of imminent delivery. He is prepared to wait until whenever it is that civilized people wait. To do otherwise would be aggressive. He is doing it for world peace.

Alas, the next diner in line is an American. The interventionist will out. He reaches over the counter and picks up Dieter's order and hands it to him.

"For me?" Dieter asks, startled.

"For you," he says.

Dieter walks out, chicken in hand, dissolving into the humid air and foot traffic on Canal Street beneath a giant fluorescent sign declaring, *"Bienvenue à la Nouvelle-Orléans. Laissez les bons temps rouler."*

— *Christian Champagne*

1:34 P.M.

OLIVIA'S GOT A SNOWBALL'S CHANCE IN HELL at ever tasting the daily special—club sandwich, fries, and Coca-Cola for only sixty-five cents. The cup of coffee sitting before her literally took an act of Congress to receive. Now it sits cold, and until today it was the only thing black the waitress had ever served. Olivia stares at the clock, just above the glass display of lemon meringue pies (sure'd be tasty with that special), and thinks it must be broken. One thirty-seven. Haven't they been here forever and a day? The waitress certainly seems to think so.

Forget the clock and look at something else, she determines, but not at her friends. Surely, they will see how weak she is—see her fear. The glass shaker of sugar goes unnoticed and so will she. Olivia sits and stares at the white crystals and tries to forget the white folks, hoping to sweeten the moment, wishing she could be as white as the sugar, if only for this minute.

It was the Reverend's fault that she was here. He'd whipped the congregation into a righteous frenzy last Sunday with his talk of "taking our place at the table." Of course Olivia clapped and sang and wept for a better seat at that table, but it was Bobby Farrell she really wanted to sit next to, and if he was willing to go to Baton Rouge and see about getting a cup of coffee, so would she.

Olivia's head-over-heels clumsy for Bobby Farrell. But it's high time for her to snap out of it, or so her mother reminds her. It is one thing to get the stupids around a boy, say, in high school. But she is two years into college and studying to be a teacher—just what kind of example will she set for her students if she keeps walking into walls every time Mister Pretty Boy comes around . . . or so her mother thinks. Well, maybe Momma's right. Surely being here in this diner right now is flirtin' with the stupids, even riskier than Bobby's "oh I love ya baby" maneuvers in the backseat of a car. But she'd gladly risk her virtue just to be away from the angry stares; hell, right about now she'd give anything just to be headed home with or without Bobby, safe at the back of the bus and this time enjoying the fumes.

Tempted as she is to see if the clock's minute hand has moved forward, she remains focused on the sugar shaker with its greasy smudges all about it and the slightly damp crust of sugar that puckers the lip of the shaker. You'd think the damn waitress could clean it now and then—sure wouldn't wanna see her home, a real pigsty she bets. Don't worry, Olivia thinks, I wouldn't wanna drink from any water fountain after you either.

Sitting stock still, despite the stool's ever wobbling tilt to the right, Olivia's bottom is numb and her feet have gone to sleep. Her neck is downright stiff from her vigilant watch over the shaker. She no longer smells the country fried steaks or the charred bits of ground beef crisping on the grill; all she smells is the starch melting from her dress. Fear pours down her back.

How much longer?

"I've waited a long time for this cup of coffee," comes a voice seated to her left. And then, just like that, a hand covers hers. A bit bony, very wrinkled, dark as earth, and etched with talcum powder, maybe Wind Song—she would smell her own hand later to find out. The sugar spell is broken. The clock will resume ticking, Bobby Farrell will continue to dog her, mature into a good husband and father, and her teaching certificate will provide a career of mentoring . . . but for now, all that matters is this old woman and the comfort of her hand. And not wanting to wait, as the old woman has for so many years, Olivia orders two slices of lemon meringue pie.

— Debbie Lindsey

1:37 P.M.

THE MASS OF PEOPLE IS STOMPING TOGETHER on the pavement, but their rhythm is retarded.

The parade is marching down Rampart Street, indolently — much like toothpaste being forced from a bottle: lots of pressure from behind forcing the movement of the parade down, what appears, a narrow passage. The street is broad but the amount of people make it confined.

The road is dirty: pollution and population. The heat is swelling the smell of sewage. No serious brushing will clean this mess.

Everyone is celebrating Martin Luther King Day a day early.

A horse clip-clops down the center median. The rider, a squat black man, holds the reins in one hand and a half-empty bottle of Jack Daniel's in the other. He tugs the reins left, then right. The horse maneuvers drunkenly, but it's not the horse, it's the rider. He takes a pull from the bottle, spilling it into his throat and slamming it down. The air is thick, but he sweats from the alcohol.

The clopping is echoing into the ears of a young black man with a natty Afro. He is walking in front of the horse. The young black man is focused on accomplishing something in his hands. The horse darts forward. The squat black man is jarred by the jolt. A dram from the bottle splatters on the pavement. The young black man scoots, agilely, to the sidewalk, claiming safety when he gets there.

He returns to the objects in his hands. There is a strike; it's a match. He lights the joint. The smell of marijuana permeates the air. It blends into the whirling smoke billowing from the lungs of a man behind him: middle-aged, bedraggled, with a blunt the size of a large carrot in his mouth. They walk together, in stride, the one behind the other, blowing smoke into the air.

Two gay men follow the footsteps of the pot-smoking men. They come together, take a deep breath of the pleasure cloud, and clench each other's hands. The one with the mustache kisses the clean-shaven, after-shave-dampened cheek of his lover. A middle-class white boy walks awkwardly along the sidewalk, on the outskirts of the parade.

Everyone's feet keep stomping, step after step, down the street, grinding and crushing grime into the crevices of the concrete. Each foot claims its position when it stamps down but knows its place. It knows it won't be there long. It will keep trudging on, right into Martin Luther King Day and beyond.

— L. Scott Connor

1:45 P.M.

THE BOY IS SITTING IN THE TERRACE of the Superdome, thirty-five rows up. The Saints are winning this Sunday, and this is quickly becoming the norm. His long, floppy blond hair brushes over the shoulder of his Dalton Hilliard jersey as he leans forward in anticipation of the next play.

A man emerges from the tunnel at the bottom of the section. He is of average height and medium build and has light brown hair. He is wearing a suit and smiling at the entire section above him, waving to everyone slowly, back and forth.

The boy realizes that this man is David Duke. What the boy knows about Duke is that he used to be in the KKK and is running for office. Duke is on the news often in the boy's home and is generally not approved of by anyone he knows.

An idea suddenly switches on in the boy's mind. As he silently commits to it, he begins to get nervous. He tells his uncle seated next to him that he'll be back in a minute as he gets up and moves past into the aisle.

The boy begins the long, thirty-five-row descent toward the average-sized man, still happily shaking hands and waving below. His heart begins to beat heavily. He quickly considers giving it up and returning to his seat.

The boy keeps going.

As he nears the bottom of the stairs, he considers walking past the average-looking man and on to the bathroom. He thinks to himself that it isn't too late to abort.

The boy steps down the last stair and onto the landing with the average man. His heart pounding inside of his sternum, the boy looks up at the man to catch his eye.

The average man sees the boy, smiles down at him, and says, "Hello." The man offers his hand.

The boy hesitates for a moment. His hands are quivering. He looks up into the man's eyes and says, "You suck."

The man's face twists up. The corners of his mouth turn down rigidly as his eyes narrow in anger. For a moment, the boy is afraid of the man's private display of naked rage.

The man withdraws his hand. The boy sees the corners of his mouth move higher as the man turns back toward the crowd. The average man begins to wave up at the section, offering a hollow, plastic smile.

— James L. Jones III

1:51P.M.

L. A. NORMA STOOD ON THE STONE FLOOR of Amtrak's waiting room, on Loyola Avenue, and blew a plume of Camel cigarette smoke into the face of a young woman named K. O. We awaited the Station Master's call for *The City of New Orleans.*

A security guard stood near the ticket desk. He held a medium-sized yellow plastic bucket. Around its lip, in three-inch red Magic Marker lettering, was "Homeland Security."

"The best thing about Bloomsday is that none climb too far out on the limb of understanding it," Norma said, as the guard pushed the yellow bucket under her chin. The bucket was filled with sand. "Smokin' ain't allowed here, lady," he said.

Norma pushed the cigarette from her lips with her tongue. It fell atop the sand with a soft plop. The guard thanked her and turned back toward the desk.

We were on our way to Jackson, Mississippi and the exhibition, "The Glory of Baroque Dresden." K. O. and her boyfriend, O. K., were on their way back home to Memphis. We had met the night before at O'Flaherty's celebration of James Joyce's obtuse novel. The bar had been crowded, it being the one-hundredth Bloomsday, and the two had squeezed in at our table.

K. O. sported purple hair, one gold nose ring, and two glass chandelier earrings made from tiny red and green crystal crosses. Her fellow traveler, O. K., was similarly colored and pierced, with six gold earrings in his right ear and one in the left. They each carried a string bag with six bottles of Stone Cellars red wine. We all watched the security guard navigating back to the ticket desk, a trail of smoke issuing from his yellow bucket.

"*The City of New Orleans,* an adventure in slow motion," O. K. said as we boarded. It wasn't clear if he meant the train or the city.

The doors clattered closed and we slipped out past the Arena and Superdome. The Superdome looked like the box the Arena had come in. At town's edge, we rocked over marshland of blue channels dotted with clumps of thick green grasses that came right up to the roadbed.

"That's the quicksand from which Tarzan was always pulling stumbling British explorers," Norma told us.

"One day the whole Big Easy will be sucked down into some giant clump of marsh grass," O. K. said, passing a wine bottle. We ate Chicago pizza in the diner and saw manmade ponds alongside the tracks. The ponds were filled with manmade catfish, watched over by long-necked white egrets. We were gliding up the gentle incline of America's old Continental Shelf.

— *Leonard Earl Johnson*

1:55 P.M.

MY OFFICE ON THE SECOND FLOOR OF CITY HALL is so big I could do a cartwheel. Not that I ever have. This is where I write letters — to be signed *C. Ray Nagin* — at a veneered, *L*-shaped desk. But right this minute I'm swiveled toward the floor-to-ceiling windows instead. It's two in the afternoon and the sky is the same drab gray as the carpet. Soon, the heavens will open up, and Poydras Street will flood all the way up to the end of the Superdome. I glance at my IN basket, which I've already been through. A family got evicted from their project apartment, a man wants to add on to his house in Tremé, a woman's son was murdered, and no one's doing anything about it. Including me.

"Why you in the dark?" The director of administration appears in the doorway; the buttons on her purple business jacket might pop any second under the force of her great bosom. When she flicks the lights on and off, it leaves long blue tracks in my vision, the same shape as the fluorescent tubes on my ceiling.

"Oh, I prefer the natural light," I say.

"Well, there isn't any today." She turns the lights on again. "Hey, when you write a letter to da guvna, use the nice paper," she advises, shaking one of the masterpieces I created yesterday on the flimsier letterhead. The guvna? Oh, the governor.

"Yeah, I'm coming," she says to someone down the hall. "You know," she says to me, "there's barbecued shrimp in there." I know about it because the director of scheduling, the finance officer, the deputy director of administration, the receptionist, the summer intern, and the guy who cleans the bathroom have already told me. I'm allergic to shrimp, crawfish too. I tell them this every time someone sends over a vat of whatever to put out in the conference room. Still, they come in every time, one by one, to ask why I'm not in there eating it.

They want to feed me because I'm a Yankee, I think. I seem a little cold, like I could use a hot lunch. They tell me I shouldn't be drinking that Diet Coke, that I need to try some baked macaroni. That'll put some meat on my bones. On my first day here, I went up to the window in that marble hallway on the first floor, where you go when you're new to get an employee ID.

"You got a Social Security number that starts with 1-9-1," said the plump man behind the glass. "Are you from New *Yawk* er somethin'?"

"Pennsylvania," I blinked.

"Hey," he yelled to his co-workers, "the new mayor's hiring *girls* from New *Yawk!*"

Well I'm sorry, but I can't eat shrimp, and I'm too sleepy to get anything done. I know the coffee maker in the kitchen isn't working, so I walk down the hall to the mayor's waiting room, where there's nice furniture and a big glass candy bowl with a gaping rim. It's been filled so high a few stray pieces have fallen around it on the dark wood table. I check to make sure no one's around, then I dig my hand down deep, separating the cheap candy from the rich chocolate by touch, judging by the smoothness of the wrappers. When I'm satisfied with my fistful, I withdraw upward, a bicep curl.

"Sweetheart," says a man's voice. I reel around. "You know we're in the middle of a budget crisis?" The mayor's head gleams. My face goes pink.

— Cristina Black

2:00 P.M.

IT'S TWO O'CLOCK ON FRIDAY and Scott Kupper is leaning on his truck parked on the corner of Railroad and Pine. It's a good location. From here he can watch for potential customers coming out of Paul's Café and tourists visiting Ole Hardhide's wire cage. Friday is alligator feeding day and Dave Opdenhoff has just served Ole Hardhide's dinner of raw chickens and driven off in the city water truck. Now Scott watches as a tall brunette in a denim skirt dashes across the railroad tracks toward him. "They're beautiful," she says, pointing to the white cardboard boxes arranged on the tailgate of his 1990 Chevy truck. Ten years ago Scott and his daddy built the metal and plywood frame that arches over this pale blue truck and Scott stenciled the red and green "Kupper Farm Strawberries" himself. The boxes are filled with strawberries . . . succulent, perfect berries every one . . . emitting a fragrance like no other in the world. "How much for a half-flat?" the woman asks. When he tells her eight dollars, she says it's a good price for mid-March. Scott smiles. It's not about the money. He's only a hobby farmer with two acres of plants behind his yellow house. He works for the Department of Agriculture, but that's not all about money either.

He's thirty-seven, quite handsome, with hair the color of rich dirt, a mustache and neatly trimmed beard to match. Straight white teeth and a ready smile. A sturdy frame; legs like fence posts. He wipes his hand on his T-shirt advertising Woody's Ukulele Shop. "Come play with us," the shirt invites passersby. Scott knows strawberry farming isn't playing. It's hard work, planting, picking, cutting, cleaning. There are the years of fighting insects, years Mother Nature sends late frosts or too much rain, the years of prices going down so low he can barely afford the plastic mulch he spreads on the field.

But, it's not all about work. There's euphoria, too, he thinks, as he offers the lady a berry to taste. Juice trickles down her chin and they both laugh. "Sweet," she says. He tells her that strawberries are the aphrodisiac he learned to love in his infancy. To Scott, strawberry farming is all about the wonder of watching something so tiny grow into a twelve-inch-high bush. A rosebush actually. Strawberries are really swollen pistils of seeds in the rose family, he tells the lady, but he knows that nobody cares about that except people like him. And his daddy, who was a bona fide strawberry farmer with twenty-five acres of straight rows you could run a plumb line down. In the 1990s his daddy set up shop on this very spot beside the railroad tracks in Ponchatoula and taught Scott that the really interesting thing about selling isn't the product, it's the people. You have to like people to sell, Scott tells his own son. You can't learn to appreciate life watching television and playing video games. You've got to get out in the fields where Mother Nature will cure your blues, he says. But Scott knows those mournful blues aren't cured so easily.

As the woman walks away carrying her box of berries like an offering, Scott looks down the tracks and swallows twice. He's standing where just last year Mama sat in a lawn chair selling her berries. She wasn't feeling so good that day, and she closed up shop and walked away. Diabetic coma, they said. Never felt a thing when she fell on the tracks just as the train came through. He pockets the five and three ones the brunette paid him and whispers, "No, it's not about the money."

— *Bev Marshall*

2:09 P.M.

THE DAY IS SUNNY and unseasonably hot in this oil-patch town of Lafayette, rejuvenated and rich again after the big "Oil Bust" of the 1980s. Mardi Gras is just past and strings of plastic beads still hang from the branches of downtown trees recently planted on a spiffy new pedestrian mall. Around the corner, the long side of a corrugated-steel warehouse is painted with a tidy yellow faux façade just big enough for a bright red door and overhang, a window, and a sign that says Odell Pottery. Inside are Bruce Odell's trophies as a three-time U.S. Pottery Olympics champion.

To the left of a showroom displaying his distinctive vessels, the potter stands outside an open-ended shed that holds shelves of pottery in various stages of completion and strange-looking contraptions that look jerrybuilt from wash pots and oil drums. In another room he has just finished demonstrating how to throw pots on a wheel.

Odell dons firemen's gloves and takes the lid off an oil-drum kiln; the heat intensifies and drops of sweat glisten on his face. His audience, sweating now, too, crowds around to look at the glazed pots inside the orange inferno. "Don't get too close!"

With immense tongs he snatches a red-hot pot from the glowing furnace and flames it with a concoction of water, corn oil, and alcohol that sprays from a metal wand. A burst of steam and fire soars high in the sky as the pot becomes a blazing torch. Quickly he moves inside to a kind of metal cradle filled with a dark damp pile of sawdust and ashes. It is pure alchemy as the pottery torch is rapidly manipulated with the wand and then buried for a moment of time only the alchemist knows. As smoke and flames billow to the ceiling and his wide grin takes on a devilish air, everyone understands why his arms ripple with muscles and his black T-shirt says "Pyromaniac."

"This is raku, invented by the Japanese. But I've invented my own color technique. Timing is crucial. If my colors don't come out just right, then I'm tempted to throw the pot at the train," he says, laughing. All at once his meaning becomes perfectly clear when with that ear-piercing wail that lures wanderers to leave home a freight train roars past the shed almost close enough to touch.

As the train rushes by, its cry vocalizing loneliness, the gloved hands carefully lift the smoking pot from the ashes and plunge it into a bucket of water. It takes less than a minute for the train to pass, and when it does, he is holding up a new creation, no longer humble gray clay, but a rainbow of glittering, metallic color forged into a crucible of beauty — magic made from fire and air and water and this Louisiana earth.

— Marda Burton

2:11P.M.

THE OLD GENTLEMEN SIT ON FRANKLIN AVENUE'S NEUTRAL GROUND in folding chairs and drink coffee and beer. They wear dress pants with short-sleeve shirts and jaunty caps. The smoke from their cigarettes rises like halos around their heads and caresses the limbs of the crepe myrtle tree above them. Occasionally, one of them gestures with a finger as he speaks and then they all throw their heads back and laugh.

The old gentlemen are the guardians of the neighborhood. You can walk up to them and ask them any question, like "Where can you buy the best men's undershirts?" or "Who's sleeping with the pastor's wife?"

And they pause for a second, stare at you, and then the guy in the Saints cap with the Miller Pony in his hand answers:

"Old Chinese guy on St. Claude near the junk store has the best price on shirts and you better talk to Eugene here about your other question."

— Donna Maria Bonner

2:22 P.M.

POSTED FADED YELLOW SIGN HANGS ON THE TERMITE-CHEWED POST in Pointe Coupee Parish. Wild wisteria vines twist into a carpet covering the porch. A wooden porch swing, with remnants of white paint, dangles from one rusted chain. A woman in full, long-sleeved white dress, beads of humid sweat formed around her lips, sits on the swing. Softly humming, gently rocking a child into a nap. A beaten swollen dark wood door has sealed itself into the threshold. Two lengthy windows are frameless and paneless. Remnants of thick lead glass twinkle off the floor. Ribbons of beaded board float down from the ceiling. Broken bricks and ash gather in the center of a crumbling chimney. A simple unadorned mantel is scarred by scratches of profanity. On the mantel rests a solitary broken figurine blackened by age and soot. A young man places his smoking pipe on a mantel tray. Chicory sweetness drifts into the room. He stoops, prods, stokes a fire for warmth, looks toward the kitchen for food. The kitchen no longer exists. The roof and walls, broken pots, scattered dish pieces lay unburied in milk thistle weeds mixed with pasture grass. A four-legged massive stove has tumbled further, into a colossal southern Oak tree with vine-covered limbs stretching over the land, into the heavens, or rotted fallen onto the earth. A long thick braided rope hangs from one limb. A young girl climbs onto the tree swing, calling for her brother to push her higher, higher. Ribbons hold the fallen bonnet around her neck, her hair flips forward, backward with each push and pull on the braided ropes. Laughter stirs the giant leaves. Which fall toward the ground in a mound of slow decay. The trunk of the tree is gouged and sunken where a limb was pulled away by storm. In the hollow rests a statue of the Virgin Mother. Her eyes chipped away by rain to become a vacant stone glare. Chips of faded blue paint cling on her robe. Her arms are stretched over the haunted grounds where families once stayed.

— *Michele Cushman*

2:30 P.M.

ON EACH SIDE OF FANNIN STREET in Shreveport, not far from Allen Avenue, half a dozen shotguns sway with each sigh of the afternoon sun. They could fall in upon themselves, be knocked over by a bulldozer making half an effort, or stand as damaged and strong as the occupants some still hold. It makes no difference to them, though standing still seems easiest somehow. The rusted metal or particle roofs threaten to spill into the bushes that squeeze between the structures. The paint, if any still remains, blisters with chronic eczema. The gray of the sinewy bones and clinging paint strips make them look more like their elderly lodgers' hair. The houses and tenants remain weakly rooted, as if in a race to stand at rest and see who lasts longer.

The electrical ropes threaten to pull them off of their foundations by their attic vents, but they don't mind. It hasn't happened yet, and they are not so worried. Overgrown plants, nearly reaching the overhangs of the porches, splay out between them, arching over and covering disjointed stairs that don't even support the ghosts whose arms no longer threaten to reach between the steps and grab at ankles that rarely ascend anymore. They are not lonely; though they sometimes wonder when a breeze from a truck with new tires drives by, slowly, if the stares should matter to them. They decide that new eyes do not matter much more than the old and they remain still. Sometimes they glance at one another, just to make sure the view hasn't changed.

A clothesline is the only suggestion of a life lived for many, stretched across the porch like the stories told there since a time they can no longer recall. One empty, detached façade shows off a white banister set against nothing. It may have been vacant for an hour or fifty years. If someone returns in a moment from whenever *now* means, that will be fine with the houses, but they won't mind if no one ever comes back to the off-kilter doors with the rusted hinges. The hinges will be there when someone is ready for them.

Not far from the hinges, colors dot the covered entrances like sprinkles on a cupcake, the lip of the cake pulling away, like siding on a house. Underneath, where the crawdads don't live and never have, there is nothing but grass disappearing into shadow and moisture. While the rest of its skin peels away, lavender mascara stares back from around the windowpanes. Colored towels are draped across shapes containing things they have never thought to uncover. But here, a woman's defiant arm and hand grasp the railing at the top, where the porch meets the steps — and the stairs, like the woman, are wearing their Saturday best: red lipstick on each of their teeth. Her arm remembers the house's name by touch and the woman glares down at the outside interruption of a camera's closing shutter. The shotgun, however made-up, is unmoved by the chance encounter.

— *Tara Scherner de la Fuente*

2:37 P.M.

SHE ANSWERS THE DOOR and greets an old friend. He's on his way to law school and wants to say good-bye. Her four-year-old daughter plays contentedly in the backyard. A calm lull descends as the aroma of red beans and rice drifts out of the open windows. White curtains breathe and ripple noiselessly. There is laughter and reminiscence.

Suddenly, a furious knocking. She darts from her puzzled guest and swings open the front door. She stares into the gnarled, weathered face of the black yardman from down the street. They've waved and greeted each other a hundred times the way neighbors do, the way yard workers politely acknowledge the ladies of the neighborhood when they come driving by. Now he has the eyes of a man possessed, muttering unintelligibly.

"I sho nuff tole 'em dey not takin' dat baby guhl!" he gasps. "I sho nuff did!"

Next to him, her small white hand clasped in his huge brown one, stands the child, trembling and crying softly.

And so it happens at a particular moment in this yardman's day—perhaps upon filling his tenth bag of leaves, or carrying the garbage to the bin, or eating his carefully packed brown-bag lunch—that he glances a few houses down and sees two strangers, a man and a woman, leading the girl to an unfamiliar car.

He had a "spookin'," he declares breathlessly. In the pit of his stomach, he knew "dem folks was up to sumptin' bad."

So he sprints down the street. He picks up a tire iron, holds it over his head menacingly, and tells the would-be abductors if they don't turn her loose, he'll "hit 'em where the sun don't shine." He is offered fifty dollars cash to look the other way and go about his business. He declines, to put it mildly. The authorities are called and a report made. The local news features the incident, warning parents to be watchful for a couple who tried to lure a child into a car.

Later, the girl will have supper and a bath, just like any other night. All around, the stirrings of tomorrow will begin. The neighborhood dogs will be brought in, and the street will get quiet. Dishes will be washed and school clothes laid out. Children will argue, then relent. There will be scurrying and hurrying about. The wail of the tugboats will echo across the Red River, their mournful sound rising and falling. And forty-five miles due south, Confederate and Union casualties of the Battle of Mansfield lie undisturbed under the silent oaks, painless and free.

Here on Earth, the rituals of the living proceed.

"Don't forget to brush your teeth."

"Where did you put my book sack?"

"Lights out in five minutes."

"Yes, ma'am."

Outside, the trees will begin to sway and take on the appearance of huge, benevolent guards standing watch. The trauma of day will ease into blessed rest. And a mother and father will kneel by the side of a bed and offer thanks for the child who was almost gone.

Across town, a tired old black man will warm up his supper, fall asleep in his rocker, and dream.

— Leslie Alexander

2:39 P.M.

SHE WAITS FOR MA-MAW to pull the gritty brown sock of dark roast from the white porcelain pot. Then she watches as the cotton-haired icon pours meager half-cups, as she does after dinner every day. Finally, her grandmother takes the butcher knife and cuts a square of melting fatback on the stained kitchen counter, where the boys left it, and ties it to the end of the string dangling patiently from the girl's hand. She is not allowed to handle knives.

Through the dining room, where the scraped bowls still sit in the afternoon light. Through the living room, where idle conversations hang in the thick smoke. Onto the front porch, where Guppy, the old Catahoula, licks a rusted pan, while Pa-Paw props his feet on the corner post, gnaws a toothpick, and looks out over his barren land. Down the steps and her feet hit the hot dirt that is Paradise, Louisiana. Navigating the great roots and sticker balls of the sweet gum tree, she quickens her pace. The boys are already out of sight. They have arrived there by now.

The honeysuckle beckons with its summer sweet, but she breaks into a run all the way to the cattle gap. There, she carefully places each foot to avoid the maze of concrete holes. Catching her breath, she traverses the gravel, which takes her ultimately to the tiny bridge of the crawdad hole that they call Flaggon Creek.

Dragonflies dance on the emerald glass water. Lush growth of green zigzags through the dead brush. The boys have left the bridge and gone down close to the water, dropping their lines in close to the magic. But she stays on the bridge.

Sitting on the edge, tucking her worn cotton dress between her legs, she drops the baited string down into the silent creek. Dipping her toes into the cool liquid, she smiles. One of the boys has thrown a handful of rocks up to make the telephone wires sing. The others condemn him for breaking the quiet.

A tug on the string. She pulls it too quickly. Part of the fatback is missing. But she will try again. This time she must watch more carefully and not be distracted by the boys. As she waits, a monarch and a buckeye play in the thicket. The heat burns her back, and the bridge warms her bottom, but something will bite soon.

The second tug. She gently lifts the string from the water. Delighted, she brings it up to her lap. The crawdad is small. He struggles at the fatback. Afraid to pet him, she whispers to him. Getting on her belly now, she looks closely into his beady black eyes. She giggles. He knows her somehow.

"What you got?" comes the shout from across the creek. She has to wink an eye to see them in the glare. When she doesn't answer them, the boys trudge up the bank toward the bridge. Still too afraid to touch and pull him from the bait, she contemplates untying the little jagged piece of fat. But Ma-Maw knows how to tie a good knot.

The boys approach the wooden planks of the bridge. She kisses the tail of the crawdad, then lowers the creature safely back into the water. As their feet pound the boards announcing the boys' arrival, she releases the string from her hand.

— Patricia Ellyn Powell

2:45 P.M.

SOMEWHERE INSIDE THE RED THREE-STORY BUILDING at the corner of St. Philip and Royal streets, children are warming up their horns, wetting their reeds, snapping on their snares. It's Carnival season, so the fifth and sixth graders in the school band are prepping once again for the school parade through the streets of the French Quarter. After they are done prepping in the band room on the third floor, the band assembles in the rear playground to practice marching. The schoolyard is hidden from the street, shaded by great magnolias and live oaks, and bounded by the brick-and-stucco back buildings—the slave quarters, kitchens, and *garçonnières*— of Creole townhouses. It smells of sweet olive, sour milk from discarded milk cartons, and Indian bidi cigarette smoke. The band leader is a large-framed, balding black man with a full beard and healthy paunch. He sweats profusely—his forehead glistens, and the underarms of his peach-colored extra-large guayabera shirt are soaked through. He's trying to light a bidi cigarette that keeps going out. It's tough because his paper matches don't stay lit long enough in the breeze. The kids call him "Mr. Payton." One of them rags him about smoking those "funny numbers" at school. He ignores it, but gives up on the skinny half-smoked Indian cigarette, fumbling it back into the worn pack in his left chest pocket. "OK, now," he says, standing up straight and surveying the band, "we lined up?" The kids, in their white band shirts (the extent of the uniform), look at each other and nod. Mr. Payton nods, too. "OK. Frank?"

Frank is the first trumpet, a mop-haired boy, one of the school's handful of white students. He nods and presses his horn to his mouth. *Dee da deeeee*—but the *da!* that's supposed to punctuate the phrase doesn't come out. He tries it again. No. Again, the last note of the "Second Line" clarion call fails to show up. The kids all look at him. Not all—some, among the woodwinds in the back, whisper and giggle about their own private matters. "Mr. Payton," Frank says. "I need some *erl.*"

Mr. Payton puts on a quizzical, confounded expression. "Whatchu say, son? Whatchu need?"

"Some *erl*. For my trumpet."

"Whatchu talkin' 'bout? For your *valves?*"

"Yessir."

"What's this about '*erl*'? Boy, you mean *awl*. Say it. Say *awl*."

"*Orl*," Frank tries it, "*ol*."

Mr. Payton reaches in another guayabera pocket and hands Frank a little plastic bottle of valve oil. Frank oils his valves and hands it back, clicking his fingers over the keys.

"OK, now," Mr. Payton says, raising his finger.

Now Frank succeeds at executing the opening solo notes of the "Second Line," and the rest of the band comes in with the melody and lurches forward on their feet. The drum corps at the rear creeps the tempo forward until Mr. Payton shouts their names and holds up his hand. They seem to know what he means: slow down. The amble continues into the narrow walkway leading from the rear playground to the parking lot to the right of the school building. This alley is always a shady canyon, sandwiched between the high walls of the school and of the close-pressed homes behind. Mr. Payton has turned to face forward and is walking with an exaggerated swagger in the hopes that the band will take their pace from him.

But another group of kids comes up the alleyway from the other direction. They don't seem to be accompanied by a teacher. They're making music, too. Beating broomsticks on cardboard boxes, pencils and pens on bottles and cans, slamming books together, and singing. *"Hey. Hey hey hey. Hey Pocky Way."*

"Wait a minute, now, whoa, hold up, the band's coming through here." Mr. Payton turns and signals to the band to stop. Then he turns to the troop of boys marching in the other direction. "Hey now, hold up. Where y'all supposed to be?" The apparent leader of the singing bunch is shirtless. He sings the loudest, switching his eye contact back and forth between Mr. Payton and the boys and girls behind him. But they keep coming on, wash past Mr. Payton, and start cutting through the ranks of the band. *"Hey!"* they half-shout, half-sing. *"Hey hey hey. Hey Pocky Way."*

"OK, OK," Mr. Payton says, calling Frank's name and a few others, attempting to corral his band. "C'mon now, let 'em through. Let the Indians through."

— *C. W. Cannon*

2:55 P.M.

DEAR EDITOR,

Feel free to edit this, or rewrite it entirely. I just thought the incident should not pass unheralded.

Thanks, Gary Thomas

We are not wannabe suicide bombers in the Sportsman's Paradise that is Northeast Louisiana. When we lose a limb to an explosive device of our own manufacture, it is accidental and occurs in the course of innocent merriment.

Consider Shane Hays, twenty-six, of Tallulah, as he and his brother-in-law embark on a Saturday-afternoon fishing expedition on a private pond in Madison Parish. The fish are uncooperative, but our intrepid pair is not deterred. Shane, you see, is prepared, thanks to a pipe bomb built from a recipe he got off the Internet. It's to stun the fish and bring them to the surface, like the miracle in St. Luke's Gospel.

The detonation, alas, is premature, and our hero loses his good right hand, although both he and his brother-in-law survive. Shane is young and will easily learn to use his left hand to repair the small engines he works on. And what a story for the grandchildren he'll have someday!

Bethany Bultman knows whereof she speaks when she writes of the motto/epitaph of the Northeast Louisiana redneck: "Watch this!"

2:59 P.M.

HE STOMPS INTO THE TINY OFFICE as he does every Wednesday, heads straight for the digital clock sitting atop her desk, and reads the large squared red numbers in a gruff voice:

"Two, five, nine. One minute, not my time yet. You can't write it down. That's the rules."

He looks at the blueberry candle burning its cloyingly sweet perfume on the desk and swivels to sternly glare at her sitting cross-legged on the floor. He climbs up on her desk chair and leans forward to blow out the candle in one forceful puff of air.

"I told you a'fore. Keep that out."

"I'm sorry. I should have blown it out before you got here. The big people like it. It makes them feel safe. That wasn't fair of me."

He climbs down off of the chair and trudges toward her. Squats down until he is eye level with her.

"The big people don't know nothing 'bout the matches making the shrimp nets go to fire from the gasoline and John still is very alone on the boat 'cause Daddy got new nets right when John's arm got broke. John says better just hurry get the shrimps out the nets off the boat fast, bye, bye, bye."

"You're right. I should get rid of the blueberry candle."

"I'm a half-trawler, but my daddy, he's a whole one."

He stands up, digs his white rubber shrimping boot into the blue threadbare carpet, spins on his heel, and plants his other bare foot in front of him to march back to the door. He pulls it shut and reaches up to hurriedly turn the deadbolt perched just above the knob three times before locking the door, counting out loud with each turn of the lock.

He stands at the door staring up at the map of Louisiana dotted with rape crisis centers tacked beside the knob. He reaches up and stabs the tiny house marked by the word *Houma,* encircled by a child's crayoned lopsided heart.

"Where is that?" she asks.

His words hush out of his mouth in a susurrus.

"Shhhhh. None the baby gators can swim in John's mouth in the heart house, none the baby gators can swim in hearts, everybody knows."

He opens and closes his mouth rapidly like a catfish, chopping his teeth loudly together upon each closure.

"John never was choking in this house, not one time in the dayshine."

He turns on his heels again in his military fashion and stomps over to her where she sits amidst cans of Play-Doh.

He digs his hand into the front pocket of his overall shorts. His bare chest exposes a clean count of four blue fingertips along the clavicle peeking out from the fold in the blue jean where the right strap hangs loose. He pulls out a bundle of paper towels and shoves his hand at her.

"Is this for me?"

"Not from me. John wants you to have it."

She unwinds the loops of carefully wrapped paper towels and uncovers a small blue crab, perfectly intact and cleaned out, carry-ing only the slightest scent of the Gulf Coast waters down the bayou. She holds it delicately in her hands as she speaks, working her fingertips over the ten blue pinching claws folded in precision around the body and poised as if to snap in front of the mouth.

"It's so clean. How did John get it so clean?"

"Ants. He put it in the ants after trawling on the boat. Came out the nets."

"Where is John? Can I thank him?"

He looks at the clock.

"Three, zero, zero. My time now. No more words for you."

He reaches out his hands for the cans of Play-Doh.

— Lee Barclay

3:07 P.M.

THE YOUNG WOMAN IS VISITING THE CEMETERY of Grace Episcopal Church in St. Francisville with her father, a tombstone conservator. They are here to repair Grace's gravestones, which have slowly been decaying over the years from the pollution coming from chemical plants up the Mississippi River. It is a brick church, built in 1827, with gothic windows, settled in the shade of oak trees covered in Spanish moss. A wrought-iron fence surrounds the grounds. It seems more like a church you'd find in the countryside of England or France, or so she thinks.

Her father scrapes moss off an angel with a chipped wing, then taps and measures a cracked mausoleum belonging to the Gilbert family. She walks the grounds, the pathways through the trees, and peers into the church through the keyhole in the front door. She finds the door unlocked and pushes it open.

She walks down the aisle, through colored shadows of stained-glass windows, toward dried magnolia leaves left on the altar. A marble baptismal font is in the corner, an angel holding its basin carefully with outstretched arms. The angel has a look on its face of steadiness and strength and its features are simple, unlike the ornate angels in the churchyard. Normally she did not particularly care for angels but this one she likes. She realizes that this is the place where she will be married.

She looks up at the arches in the ceiling, knowing this fact, and then the iron lanterns that hang from it, knowing it. Even the angel knows.

She is still many years from the age of marriage but she holds the thought in her mind, like the angel its basin, imagining walking through the churchyard in a wispy, long dress and carrying lilies from her mother's garden. She walks down the aisle with her father, dressed in his best summer suit, his white linen one. There would be a small picnic party for her family on the riverbank afterward.

When she reaches the altar the fantasy stops. She can't fill in the picture anymore because she can't imagine the husband to be. She can't even make him into a blur temporarily, for the sake of the day-dream.

She forgets these thoughts about her marriage, not even really aware of the obstacle to them, and goes back to the churchyard to help her father with the tombstones.

— Minter Krotzer

3:12 P.M.

THE OLD MAN SITS ON THE PORCH of his country home in Paulina, with his hound dog, Perique, by his side. It is the sugarcane harvest, a very busy time of the year. They have burned the fields, once brilliant green as far as the eye can see. The wagons are lined up along the road waiting to haul the cane to the refinery down in Gramercy. He looks forward to the harvest. With all the activity, the days are not so long.

The old man crosses the dusty road to the fields to cut a few stalks. He brings them home and stands them on the porch. Later, when his company comes, he will pull out his favorite knife and peel back the outer layer of the cane, slicing the sweet sugar chew to share. A custom passed on through the generations, the chew and the memories it brings are still sweet.

His granddaughter attends LSU, where her parents met as students. They've come down for the big game and to visit with him. Since Mama passed, they have begged Papa to come live with them. But he can't leave his home. He was born here. Besides, he is content with his constant companion, Perique.

So, he sits and waits for the visit, looking out across the sugarcane fields to blue skies and white billowing clouds. Season to season, he watches the sugarcane grow, and he awaits the harvest.

— Lina Hutches Beavers

3:15 P.M.

HIS HEART KNEW MUCH EARLIER THAN HE DID that the past was lost.

He used to sit on this stair landing, listening to the sleepers of the house, to the susurrus of their dreaming lips, and he'd well with sadness for his children's impending passage into adolescence, adulthood. Even now he still dreams of each child as a youngster — no matter how angular and rough-chinned a man or how lithesome a woman.

His walk through the gutted house, freed of the tangled mass of his moldy and shattered family life, in a neighborhood without neighbors, brought back the taste of other losses, which appeasing memory had rendered bland and indistinct.

His mother was old, and it could be said that she had lived a good long life. A half-truth that he shouldn't have relied upon, yet did. And his father died fifteen years earlier, sedated to ease his slow, painful sinkage into nonbeing. Nonbeing plainly demarked with one last agonal breath. And his mother, off life-support systems, which had bruised her arms and scratched her trachea, faded behind her old frightened eyes and receded into death. He had placed his hand on her forehead and whispered that she should remember how much the grandchildren loved her and how much fun they had together on their family trips to exotic places: Rome, Paris, Amsterdam. "Remember," he faltered. "Remember how much fun we had."

What did she hear? he wonders. What did she think?

He's hot in his disposable coveralls, rubber gloves, and respirator. His glasses are fogged beneath his goggles. He removes the goggles, mask, and gloves. His hands, starting to spot with age, resemble his father's big-knuckled ones. His fingers, so much like his father's, touch his forehead, but he feels his mother's.

— Wayne McGaw

3:22 P.M.

HE WEARS AN OLIVE-GREEN ARMY JACKET with a Purple Heart pinned above his name. *Arceneaux* is stenciled in military lettering, black, crude, like the heading on a kid's science project. Shadows of long-gone sergeant stripes still show on the sleeves. Motor-oil stains seep like wounds through the material. His pants are filthy workman's khaki, cuffed but frayed. Military dress shoes are highly polished and black as ink. The right pant leg is gathered and cinched in the jaws of a dog collar to protect it from a missing chain guard on his bicycle. His hair is gray and short, not disciplined enough to be a flattop, but longer than a burr. Scars cover his face, some too deep to be from acne.

He dismounts the bike, engages the kick stand, and scans the area in front of the convenience store. Located in Port Allen, the store is just a width-of-the-Mississippi River away from the state capitol.

Customers, filling their tanks, provide cover and diversion from the watchful eyes of the Vietnamese clerk inside the store. Timing is right; his mission is a go. He crouches behind a blue trash barrel that smells like road kill and proceeds to rifle through its contents, separating crawfish heads, half-eaten fish sandwiches, and napkins soaked in ketchup from other, more valuable, items. Flies swarm, land, and retreat from his swatting hand, only to land again. Extracting aluminum cans of Budweiser, Coke, A&W, Pepsi, and Red Bull, he drains, crushes, and squeezes the cans into a plastic bag. Heavy, worthless glass bottles of Dixie and Abita Beer are quietly returned to the barrel.

Within seconds, he loads the half-filled bag into a Red Flyer wagon attached by a rawhide strap to the seat post of the bicycle and pedals onto the shoulder of Highway 415 and then onto Interstate 10. The next exit is eight miles away.

— Mark David

3:29 P.M.

WE PASS FIELD UPON FIELD of tall, green, slender stalks of sugarcane, the border of the maze into Evangeline Parish. Roads glazed with a residue of red clay wind us through Mamou, past Ville Platte, and north of Pine Prairie. Suddenly the scenery turns from dark shades of vert sugarcane to sun-bleached cotton, and the crimson brick clay that lightly dusted the pavement becomes backdrop to the buds of cotton in the fields. The sun is blazing high, and humidity drapes itself on the collar of Majeeda's blouse.

Majeeda veers the car over to the side of the road and turns off the engine. Slowly she opens the driver's door, and carefully steps out of the vehicle. She is mindful of stirring up the dust onto her slightly wrinkled linen suit. Her steps are slow and deliberate. With determination she places one hip forward and drags the other. Unsteadily, but with great effort, she approaches a soft fluffy pillow of cotton hanging on a branch. Majeeda's dark molasses skin contrasts sharply with the field of pallid cotton blooms. Her long tendrils of dreads, perfumed with essential oils and incense, slowly graze her face as she leans down gently to touch the cloud of cotton puffs. She spreads the cotton between her fingers, and thumbs the cottonseeds in her hand as if they were rosary beads for a moment of reverent contemplation. A smile suddenly erupts across her face as she pinches off a single bloom of cotton from the branch, the color in her apple cheeks more vibrant than the rouge milieu of clay.

— Autumn Snyder Harrell

3:38 P.M.

IT IS A PERFECT SPRING (SUNSHINE-SHINES-AS-PUFFY-WHITE-CLOUDS-SPOT-THE-BLUE-SKY) AFTERNOON. The sun beats down on the fish bones, the tiny swimming tadpoles, the empty shells, the insects, the wet earth below, and you.

Earth and rock crunch beneath your feet, through your deep breathing. Small fish reflect the sky above off silver skin and swim in pools around carcasses of dissected crabs mingling with decomposing gills. Crickets, frogs, and their muddy counterparts make themselves known with song and movement. On each side of you beyond shrubs and small trees, birds float past on unseen waters. They glide along perfectly still as if on conveyer belts.

A lone road stretches behind dotted with rubbish and lined with oil refineries. Smoke billows out of the trees. A low hum comes from the refineries. The machinery growls, burps, and then grows quiet. The sounds around the still water can be heard. Insects abound, buzzing, small dropdropdrops, and in the weedy growths always a slight rustle. A snake?

There is heavy moist air cradling you as you close your eyes. Opening them and standing back up a strange and giant bird as tall as you (taller even? is that possible?) flies by and stands in the shallow water a few feet away. She watches you watching her. The black eyes behind large beak stare unflinchingly as you stare back. You look closely and then lower your head. Starting to laugh you are stifled as she reprimands you with a splash of her foot. There is no laughing. She splashes the water with her foot again. You shift your weight and she starts bwaa-*ooh*-icking, bwaa-*ooh*-icking, bwaa-*ooh*-icking and flies away.

You look out at the spidery network of water and swamp before you. You can go no further. Before you shallow waters intermingle freely with swamp grass and trees. A few feet behind you a sign notes that this is the southernmost point of Louisiana in Plaquemines Parish. You stand even past that sign. You are standing at the end of the world.

— *Karissa Kary*

3:41P.M.

THE CLOUDS ARE CRUSHED PEARLS above the marble statue of Touchdown Jesus, which stands in the lawn in front of Loyola University. From his pedestal, Touchdown presides over traffic on St. Charles Avenue, and over Audubon Park, where bikers and joggers circle in black spandex and colored shorts.

In the park, a man and a girl sit on the bank by the pond. A few feet to their right, a boy in a blue Cubs cap side-arms bread onto the water. The man, wearing jeans and a polo, lounges on an arm and contemplates the golfers beyond the far side of the pond. The girl sits upright in a peasant skirt that is tucked tightly around her knees, and her eyes follow the ducks as they paddle after pieces of bread floating among knots of Spanish moss that have fallen from the oaks. A tattered copy of *The Branch Will Not Break* rests in the grass beside her.

"So that's it?" she says or asks.

"Yes."

"And what about me? What will I do?"

As the man abandons the golfers and turns toward her, a chocolate lab ambles by, on its way to another tree. Its leash trails like a snake among the acorns on the ground.

"You'll graduate," the man says. "You'll get old."

The girl lifts her arm slowly and considers her watch. Then she says that this will be the moment when she began to hate him. She says her hatred will be fire. As she speaks, the boy in the Cubs cap flips the last of the bread onto the water and turns toward home. He imagines the runners and riders to be a river, and the gaps that he waits for will be steppingstones. Horns argue on the avenue, and a bronze butterfly flickers on Touchdown's shoulder. Now a breeze carries it away.

— *Bruce Henricksen*

3:42 P.M.

LET'S GO BACK TO THE OLD WAY.

But she doesn't remember the old way. There is only a small tent covering the burial site. She is left to her thoughts and memories as family members slowly trickle away. The hot Louisiana rain falls thin as whisper, ruining her tight curls. There is no professional runner that leads to her grandmother's resting place. The heels of her $200 BCBG are sinking deep into greenish mud.

There is no plush limo to drive them to the gravesite. There's no need. She's been in California so long that she's gotten used to cemeteries with stately mausoleums where the director can look out over beautiful rolling hills and see his many patrons. Where the lawns are manicured and you can only visit on certain days and certain times.

She has forgotten a little church down in DeRidder, Louisiana. Now she stands in the middle of her history. Looking around and she sees all her family right here. Great-Aunt, Great-Uncle, Grandfather, and Cousin. Some headstones so old and rotted that they are broken and a skeleton can be seen emerging like a bad B movie. No director is there to send a caretaker to fix it. It sits exposed like her past come to haunt her. She looks at the destroyed clothing. Her feet sinking so low in the mud she seems to be barefoot. Her eyes fall on the coffin of the woman she ran from so long ago. The community she shunned. The simplicity she detested. And she hangs her head in shame.

— Carolyn Wysinger

4:05 P.M.

THE ROVING EYE, ALL-SEEING, BRAINLESS, having roved over Rome, Paris, New York, London, Venice—San Francisco soon to come—opens now again upon New Orleans, fixes upon the standing violinist and the seated guitarist at the curb just outside Café du Monde. The camera eye craves the young woman bent over the mouth of her guitar, but favors the violinist, standing tall, straight, ankles crossed, an iron pole a second spine, a flowing scarf draped over her left shoulder, tucked under the violin, one toe poised like a ballet dancer's pointe.

The peripatetic eye does not have tourist, alien vision only, domestic vision, too, but, after decades, is weary of opening to New Orleans sights. But the eye cannot resist this cliché in this manifestation, the standing Asian young woman is so perfect, so still, so elegant, except for the arm that is making music, strange and galvanizing.

The open eye waits until two small young Asian women wearing caps that declare Café du Monde frame the violinist. About to shutter the image, the eye sees, rising from a group just under the tent, obstructing the view, a young woman, long, swaying mane of blond hair accenting her sleeveless, short black dress. Stepping out of her North Dakota family group—father flanked by wife and daughter left sitting poker straight behind their beignets and coffee—the woman in black thrusts her body toward the tall violinist, takes up a spread-legged stance, lifts her lithe arms, begins to sway very slowly, stepping closer in a graceful crouch, then backward, straightening, back and forth, mane swaying, an almost aggressively adulatory dance. Adored, the violinist gazes into her eyes.

The lioness looks back over her shoulder at her family, each one stiff, resistant, until the mother lifts her arms, begins to sway to the music, to her daughter's intensely focused dancing, but stays seated.

The lioness's dance obstructs the camera eye's view of the violinist, fragments the alignment of figures.

At last, the lioness waves goodbye to her mother, her father, her sister, and crosses the street with the air of rushing to meet someone, oblivious of the mime in Scheherazade costume on the opposite curb.

The camera lids its eye, capturing the statuesque violinist, and sighs.

At rest on its closet shelf, emptied of its roll, the camera cannot stop remembering the dancer it wishes—too late—it had taken.

—David Madden

4:25 P.M.

THE IRONING BOARD IS STANDING, pulled down from the hanging hook behind the door of the employee restroom. In the storage room, among plastic bins of flour and cases of peeled tomatoes, with careful fingers folding and leading the fabric of his shirt under the iron, a man in a fragile, quiet body and black dress pants bends at the waist, concentrating on the creases he is pressing into his shirt sleeves. Breathing through his mouth, he shifts his feet in a slow syrupy dance around his work. Each time he rights the iron, it sighs and his shoulders relax away from his ears for the few moments it takes to arrange his shirt to another position. As he drops his cindered head and raises his shoulders, laundry steam cleans the air of the dreary dust and cardboard scents that accompany a restaurant's pantry.

With stomping feet and rumbling words in rhythm escorting him, a young kid with braids and small eyes charges around the corner and flops into a chair several feet in front of the lanky waiter peacefully starching his uniform. A dishwasher, the kid dries the chemical water from his hands on his gumbo-stained pants and rummages in the sagging pockets for a Swisher Sweet cigar. He measures the smooth movements of domesticity across from him as he pops his lighter and bounces his head to music only he can hear. After drawing a couple of drags off the plastic tip and replacing the peaceful smells of fabric softener with dirty candy smoke, the dishwasher leans forward, elbows on knees. Gesturing with the cigar tucked into his palm between thumb and forefinger, he cocks his braids and asks, "Say, brah. You like doin' that?"

The waiter raises only his eyes to him for a moment, then shrugs. "I like lookin' good, lookin' tight," and he flips the shirt to the other sleeve. Sigh. Steam. Silence.

"Who taught you that? Yo' mamma?" and the dishwasher pulls smoke again, his eyes tucked back and guarded, his voice edged with testy humor.

"No," the shirt capes over the waiter's back for a moment as he points one arm, then the other through the sleeves and begins to button up over his undershirt, "the army." The dishwasher grins wide, his chin to the ceiling.

"I got it, man. I got it. You iron the other guys' shirts 'round here—charge 'em, say, five bucks each. I'll hustle the business, like your agent, you know, advertisin'. Then we split it fifty-fifty. Two fifty each. Whatchu think?" Leaning back in his chair, he shows his teeth and bounces his eyebrows.

"I think you hustlin' me, brah. That's what I think," says the waiter with kind eyes and a mouth of mirth. Metal scrapes and rips as the waiter collapses the board and props it against the wall.

The dishwasher's eyes retreat as he slouches back in his chair and responds, "I'm just a businessman, brah." With eyes closed and his head too heavy to hold up, he adds, "Always lookin' for an opportunity."

— Julia Carey

4:29 P.M.

THE CATHOLIC FAITHFUL ARE GATHERED in St. Joseph's Church in Marksville on a cold gloomy February afternoon for Mass. This is the senior Mass, largely attended by the geriatric set, sixty and older, with a smattering of youth and younger couples. Even though the weather is dreary, the church is filled. A couple is in a pew near the middle of the church with a dark-haired boy standing between them. The boy closely resembles his father. The priest reads another intercession. "Give every grace and blessing to our married couples. . . . Help them to grow in understanding, patience, and true love. . . . Make them outstanding role models for their children and youth. . . . We pray to the Lord." The boy suddenly becomes alert then looks up at his father on his left, then up toward the woman on his right, his stepmother. As the intercession continues, he reaches out and takes his father's hand in his left hand, and his stepmother's in his right, and then looks at both again, joining the couple to each other through himself.

— *Theresa Thevenote*

4:45 P.M.

PAST THE COW PASTURES and the soybean crops and the bridge where Bayou Teche and Bayou Fusilier meet, around the corner from Arnaudville's single grocery store, in back of the warehouse that was once a gym, you spend a minute checking for snakes. Then you strip.

You are careful to angle the scrap of curtain around the makeshift shower so you are concealed from anyone to your right. That is where the do-it-yourself carwash is, and beyond the carwash, a ways down Highway 31, is the crackhouse. The crackheads are always walking the highway to buy crack from the men who wash their cars for hours all day and night. They have worn their own path into the gravel that is your front yard. You live in an abandoned store with a microwave and mattress but no shower. Sometimes the crackheads stop and ask you for beer until you lie and say it's all gone away. You have seen it in their eyes, this unrestrained hunger; you are just another thing they would consume if they could.

Today the water smells a bit like rotten eggs with a chemical edge to it, kind of like Nair, you think, and wonder if the soapy carwash water has mixed in with your water supply. The cement is slippery beneath your feet from bars of soap left to dissolve next to empty shampoo bottles. These Cajuns you've met, they are kind enough to let you use their shower. They were kind enough to smile when you confronted them about what they did to the shower curtain, how they lowered it so that if you stand up straight, the bayou has a clear view of your breasts. You are not worried about the Cajuns today; they've gone offshore. They'll return in two weeks to spin their tires out on the highway and drink Coors Light while talking about what work can do, their eyes the only things left on them unweathered by ocean, sun, and deck. Sometimes there are boys in boats who have heard the legend of you—a naked woman who lives in an abandoned daiquiri shop and showers outside—and you listen for the sound of their boat.

You are careful to clean the wound from when a dime seared itself to your knee as you rooted around in your car. The blister pops and clear liquid runs out. You had expected pus, something dirty as the bayou that reeks of dead fish. As you shave your legs a breeze whips the curtain around you and you miss a few places. You are always missing things and trying to ignore it. Your new fleur-de-lis tattoo puckers with mosquito bites and you smack at them, thinking only that to scratch would be divine until you think you will lose your mind. You realize you know how the crackheads feel.

A lizard darts past you, shocking you into an upright position. The boy is there now, pretending to fish with a stick and some string. Your breasts glisten from the water. He smiles. And then you wave.

— Tara Jill Ciccarone

5:01P.M.

FOR DAYS HE HAS BEEN SEARCHING FOR HER, from one establishment, one owner, one employee to another in the French Quarter. It is afternoon, late afternoon. "Excuse me. Do you know or have you seen the Duck Girl around here lately? She usually wore an old floppy, white, brimmed hat, white evening dress, with pink ribbons around her wrists and waist. She wore black heels that were entirely too large, that never fit, clonking along the sidewalk. Eight or ten ducks would be quacking along behind her. A marvelous procession. Have you seen her?" An elderly lady, a bit plump, wearing a white, cotton dress, with sky blue eyes, glasses that have fallen slightly down her broken nose, at one of the fruit stands in the French Market, finally responds positively. Peering over her glasses as she wipes the apples and oranges with an old rag, she says, "I don't know no Duck Girl, but there's this little lady we call the Duck Lady 'round here sometimes." "Have you seen her lately?" he asks. "No. But she wanders all over the place all the time. Over on Ursulines a lot, Dauphine, 'round there a lot." He turns abruptly, without even thanking her, as she continues, "You shorely look spiffy in that tuxedo, mister. You been to a wedding or something?" He is walking hurriedly toward Ursulines, with his seven-and-seven in one hand and his Montecristo cigar in the other, thinking *No. Just burying some friends, thank you.* Then, beyond Bourbon along Ursulines at Dauphine, as he turns and glances toward Canal Street, he sees a petite figure coming toward him, on the other side of Dauphine. He crosses the street and waits, sips from his seven-and-seven. She is wearing a broad-brimmed, tan hat, a lovely white, silk blouse, a tan, light cotton skirt, and expensive white heels that fit. Her face is still thin, weather worn and mousy, and she is still far from being physically attractive. "Excuse me," he says, ". . . aren't you the Duck Girl?" She stops and stares into his eyes, then her eyes wander off. She is thinking, as if she is trying very hard to place some incident, perhaps a few passing moments in time and space.

She almost remembers. "I didn't have a mustache then," he says, touching his mustache from habit, anxiously trying to help her remember, wanting so much to apologize to the right person. "It was twenty years ago. I was the guy who taunted you so. Held traffic up for you. Toasted you. Followed you along the streets and sidewalks, whispering lines of great poetry in your ears. Yeats, Cummings, and Keats. You never once glanced aside, never once spoke one word to me." Her eyes turn back to his, as if to touch Earth one final time. "Yes . . . I am," she says. "What happened to the ducks?" he asks, forgetting his apology. Her eyes meet his again, then wander off toward the same gray, dark, ominous sky that hung over Pat O'Brien's and so many other streets and places twenty years before, then back to his troubled face. "One day," she says, trying desperately to remember, her eyes falling now toward the cracks in the sidewalk, the shadows of late afternoon, "one day . . . they just stopped . . . following."

— Lenny Emmanuel

5:12 P.M.

CLARK, OWNER OF HIGHLAND COFFEES, is chastising his newest recruit next to one of the enormous coolers in the back. Their whir muffles his already soft words. It seems that the new girl has misplaced an inventory list. She pulls it out from behind a retired cash register and declares, "It was right here, in plain sight." Half-smiling, Clark turns away from her and begins to explain to another employee, a gaunt student poet, the difference between *this* fine-ground coffee and *that* fine-ground coffee.

The girl re-enters rotation behind the counter. Her mouth flutters with confidence. In two short and long weeks, as weeks always get near the end of a semester, her flying blond curls have already earned her a following among the coffee shop's young male patrons. Two of them, positioned strategically on leather recliners across from the counter, steal glances at her in order to time their refills. Today, it's not as easy to track her down. Her usually conspicuous hair is locked in a tight bun — she wishes to go under the radar.

The last remains of daylight seep through the live oaks lining the northern edge of Louisiana State University campus. Notebook screens glow brighter and sharper in the drowsy light from the hemispheric bodies hovering over wall mirrors and paintings of local artists. The larger of the two lounges in the coffee shop now looks like a curious cross between a powder room and a stage populated by solitary typists, news addicts, chess fiends rubbing their brows, colleagues content to sip and stare, and a few coffee-shop regulars navigating the space between tables, extending greetings.

Among the regulars is Emerson Bell, the painter who, rumor has it, hung out with Picasso's last lover. His sinewy hand clutches an English professor's shoulder. The words "piss" and "love" fly out of his otherwise indiscernible rumble. A librarian type in close proximity winces, looks up from his screen, makes a point of wincing again. But Bell's last word stays in the air, spins like a languid whale in the soft light, sprinkles abashment into the faces of students, mild surprise into the expressions of older folks. It even threatens to unfurl a flood of cascading blond curls—but doesn't.

The headlines for February 14, 2006, make no mention of New Orleans.

— Plamen Arnaudov

5:18 P.M.

IT HAPPENS AGAIN like an Ella Fitzgerald recording that skips.

She is late for her mother's fried chicken and splashes of succotash pooled in butter on blue willow plates. Gentilly dirt embeds itself against her fingers and in the curved crevices of her lifelines. Scattered among pert leaves are blossoms smaller than pin pricks. The scent rises, calls her home, and beckons Venus to appear. Moths hover. The silent flicker of wings brushes the amber porch light. Beneath the palest end of indigo is the reoccurrence of her sweet olive dream.

— Gina Ferrara

5:21P.M.

THE GREASE IS CRACKLING HOT in the iron skillet in the oven, ready for the cornbread batter to sizzle as it is poured in. The turnip greens that filled the sink in a huge pile have now shrunk in the bubbling pot on top of the stove. Bits of juicy ham hock and onions flavor the pot liquor that is ready to be dipped into and sopped with the crunchy bread when it comes from the oven.

— Margaret Truly

5:27 P.M.

ON A TYPICAL MONDAY NIGHT, roughly half past five, in Shreveport's Strawn's Eat Shop, Too there are somewhere around two dozen people lazily chatting and settling down to eat a greasy home-cooked southern meal. The walls are covered in murals of "The Andy Griffin Show," great thinkers and celebrities, even the mascots of all of the high schools and colleges in the area sitting around a table eating some of Strawn's famous strawberry icebox pie. It is set up as a fifties-style diner, with a counter and barstools to sit and eat while watching the cooks prepare the food on the long grill behind it, and wooden booths stretch along the far wall.

At the counter, sitting on two barstools, are a brother and sister, probably around four and five years old, blond and pale. They sit with burgers, sharing a large plate of fries and an even larger plate of ketchup between them. Each takes a crayon and colors a blank page, nothing particular, just scribbling to make sure the page isn't white.

There is a group of young girls, with Caddo Magnet High soccer uniforms on, sitting around one of the tables in the center of the restaurant. They are all enjoying large plates of chicken fingers and mashed potatoes, some with white, some with brown gravy. Their long hair is pulled back tightly in ponytails, cheeks still red and flushed from what was probably a hard practice in the wind and cold. They talk loudly and laugh as one girl tells a story of stealing the ball from the city's high scorer and kicking the winning point in last week's game.

And over in a corner booth, away from everyone else in the restaurant, is an elderly couple one could easily miss. They sit there almost saying nothing to one another, quietly watching the rest of the diner as they eat grilled chicken and green beans off of the same plate. The old man sips his coffee and turns to ask his wife if she is almost done, reminding her that he can't see well once the sun goes down and that they don't want to miss the six o'clock news. She smiles and says yes, so he scoots out of the booth and leans down, taking her hand to help her slide out and stand. She leans over and plants a kiss on his left cheek. He smiles as he helps her out, and they walk hand in hand to the counter to pay for their meal.

— Jada Hendrix

5:30 P.M.

IN THE FADING LIGHT of a July afternoon down Louisiana 1, close to where the land gives way to the Gulf and a sulfurous scent tints the air, a group of white-haired men sits chattering on a rusted array of metal chairs beneath thick branches cluttered with out-of-state license plates, crab traps, life preservers, and campaign paraphernalia from elections long passed.

They hardly look up as two female cyclists approach. *"Bonsoir,"* one of the women announces with some trepidation in the French she picked up during a college semester abroad.

"Where you from, Canada?" Robinson Guidry asks in his thick Cajun brogue between thick bites of scarlet watermelon. "No," the woman says, "we came from Thibodaux."

It might as well have been another country. "Come sit," Guidry offers, his face lit with the story it's clear he's more than glad to share.

"If you want to find out some news, come here. If he don't know, he knows or he knows," he says, pointing in turn to each of the men seated beside him. "That's why my wife calls it the gossip tree."

A wooden sign posted to the trunk of the tree proclaims it the Chêne à Cowan, or turtle's oak in Cajun French, a few of the men explain when asked.

"That's Cowan there," Guidry announces, pointing to the man seated at the center of the circle, a shrimper and peddler of concrete house risers now in his mid-seventies. It was he who some twenty years ago started this ritual when he pulled a chair out under the tree in his front yard to peel the yields of a trawling trip. This Guidry recounts as Antoine "Cowan" Gisclair rocks his chair back and forth with his white rubber shrimp boots.

Asked how he spells name, Gisclair reports that he can't read or write. "I mark my name with an X," he says. "Got my education other ways."

"Don't let that fool you," says a man at the back of the group, directing his gaze upward.

Smiling broadly through his thick tuft of beard, Gisclair says, "As they say around here, 'You'd better do some stumpin' at the Chêne à Cowan.'"

"Buddy Roemer came here, Edwin Edwards came here," Guidry says, gesturing toward the photos of politicians from town council-men to congressmen that litter the tree's boughs — weathered rem-nants of white-bean suppers held around election time.

"We're like 'The Oprah Winfrey Show,'" he says. "They have people from Holland come over here. *National Geographic* came over here." He pulls from his wallet a business card from the news-magazine as proof of his claims.

"This tree here's the most popular place they have on all the bayou."

— *Emilie Bahr*

5:34 P.M.

"I BET YOU WON'T RUN INTO THE FIELD."

Andrea looks to the sugarcane, its tops protesting the muggy New Iberia breeze. In them, she hears her grandfather smoothing newspaper to examine the weather report. She hears a hundred parishioners thumbing through hymnals. "Sure," she says in an off-hand way and doesn't look at her husband. They stare at the field, seeing nothing.

Robert smiles. "Aren't you afraid bugs will get on you?"

The wooden picnic table creaks under their weight, its bench their footrest. The setting sun warms their backs and casts a spotlight on the cane. Andrea heaves herself off the table and begins walking to the street.

"Why wouldn't I do it?"

"Ever did it before?"

"That field's just background."

"Do it, then."

"Just run in and out?"

"Yeah."

Andrea begins her walk toward the rows of sweet stalks. She picks a row. She sees her path. She will run into the comforting hollows, into the soft hideaway of childhood. She will lose herself for just a moment and then dash back. Robert stays steps behind, waiting for her to turn.

Behind them, a crowd's muffled roar swells. Someone has opened the door to a house full of relatives talking, with exaggerated emotions, about nothing and everything. Andrea's grandfather stands under the carport. Curious, he calls out to them. "Where're y'all going?"

Squinting into last gasps of sunbeams, Andrea hollers back, "Robert bet me I wouldn't go run into the field, Papaw, so we're going do that real quick." Next to her, Robert is silent.

"Oh, no," Papaw replies, gently scolding. His voice is low, but the French of his vowels flows across the acre between them. "The leaves will cut you like razors."

Andrea turns to Robert, air between them dead. He snorts, unable to hold back laughter. She stares at him, not knowing yet to be angry. "You knew that?"

"You didn't?" Robert tries to swallow his humor and fails. "Well, I wasn't going to really let you do it."

They walk back to the house, to the door Papaw holds open for them, his stray children returning to the fold.

— Andrea Watson

5:39 P.M.

UP NORTH A WAYS, near but not in Covington, Dr. England and his wife have a house out in the woods where he would play often. He went up there only when his dad and folks had a party to go to but Dr. England threw enough parties that he went pretty often.

There is a creek about a mile from the stables where he and all the children couldn't wait to go as they sat in their swimsuits, shivering, on the porch. They had to wait for Ms. Barbara, who with a cigarette in one hand, light beer in the other, and a lawn chair miraculously juggled between the two, steps out onto the porch and calls out, "All right, some of you boys come here and help me. Vincent, you get my beer. . . . Ben, you take the chair."

Ms. Barbara leads the children through the dark woods that seem to spread out forever with only the occasional dirt road or cabin spotted about their surface. The children make it to the creek and look out to the familiar grove where the water is deepest. The rivulet inches through the forest with a modest, determined stream. The sound of songbirds, so deep and defined in the forest's darkness, becomes a muffled whisper as he runs toward the sandbar that splits the creek into two. Ms. Barbara lights up another Marlboro and drags the lawn chair into the middle of the sandbar, where she calls out like the queen of the mountain, "Hey . . . hey . . . y'all know the rules. Boys on one side. Girls on the other."

The children split in orchestration and dive into the cool, clean water. He sits a moment on the sandbar and watches Ms. Barbara as she smokes and points toward a rabbit watching the commotion at his once-peaceful drinking spot. Ms. Barbara sits in gigantic proportion above him when she pulls out a book with a pink hardcover and begins to read. She does not look at the boy now so he stands up and begins to walk over to the girls' side, where they stare at him with full white eyes and territorial scowls.

He continues down the stream a bit longer, knowing that Ms. Barbara cannot see him now, and lets his feet drag through the sand of the bank. It is soft sand, spotted black and yellow, and he finds it feels good between his toes. The crickets begin to chirp, singing of the night to come, and he walks on until he finds that the creek comes together as one again. With a quick gesture of glee, he sits where the two streams meet, and as the water whirls and gushes around him, he chants to himself a song he heard at church but no longer remembers the words.

— William Vail

5:41P.M.

SHE STEPS OUTSIDE THE HIDEOUT, a Decatur Street dive, and into the crowd of bead-wearing, go-cup-carrying conventioneers who should have been cut off an hour ago. The sound of zydeco pours from the open doors of souvenir shops and just a few steps down the banquette, she sees him.

Gutter Punk.

Street Rat.

Invisible to most, the boy sits on the dirty, cracked sidewalk wearing yesterday's clothes and strumming a melancholy tune on his guitar. But he is not invisible to one whose heart beats forth the rhythm of a mother. Notice the unnoticeable. Love the unlovable. Her own son is a musician.

She kneels beside him. Green eyes connect to blue. The world around them is silenced, replaced with his song to no one. He smiles when it is over, his teeth as decayed as the city where he sought refuge, but found none. He tells her that he wrote this song a few days ago, and that he is tired of this place. He is ready to go home. He hopes to leave tomorrow.

She touches his cheek, places a dollar in his battered guitar case. One last glance and she walks away in the direction where her friends wait.

Escaping the crowd, she turns on Ursulines. Halfway to Chartres, a red-headed delivery boy jogs to catch up with her. They walk together for a couple blocks toward her destination in silence. Finally he speaks.

"Thank you for listening to his song."

— Dawn High McFarland

6:00 P.M.

THE TWO EIGHTEENTH-CENTURY BUILDINGS TOUCH with the uncomfort-able familiarity of strangers in an elevator who have nothing in common. One is refined; the other, a mess.

The elegant building values privacy: its shutters locked, treasures hidden. There is a Rembrandt etching in the bathroom; rare porce-lains line the dining-room wall; Impressionist paintings are in the living room. Constant face-lifts have erased the telltale signs of time: its complexion is smooth. The dog enjoys bottled water from a crystal bowl and has a monogrammed collar.

Paint peels like a week-old sunburn off of the slob next door. Its plaster skin is flawed with age spots; window units protrude and distort its face. Once, it too was home to a family, but now it is divided into nine rental units; a colony of transients comes and goes at all hours like ants. The cat on the second floor drinks out of the toilet and tortures mice.

Every night, promptly at six, as the bells from nearby St. Louis Cathedral chime, the shutters of the elegant building open; the cat jumps the wrought-iron railing that separates the two worlds and walks inside. Moments later he returns home with a treat in his mouth — tonight it is butterfly shrimp — and the shutters close.

— *Jeanie Blake*

6:01P.M.

TO MARK THE TRADITIONAL BREAKING OF THE FAST that no one keeps but Daddy, Nanny has six-foot-tall Miss Corinne serve dinner. Under the glass chandelier at the mahogany table, the family dishes up fresh-shot roasted duck, stewed okra and Creole tomatoes, and rice and gravy from silver trays and bowls. "Don't swallow thuh beebee pellets!" Nanny warns as she eyes the duck on their plates. To the brother and sister, finding a beebee is finding a prize after the long season of prayers.

They had prayed really hard since *Rosh Hashanah*, the Jewish New Year. *Avinu Malkenu* our Father our King, Hear Our Voice. *Avinu Malkenu* our Father our King, Make an End to Sickness. *Avinu Malkenu* our Father our King, Make an End to War. *Avinu Malkenu* our Father our King, Make an End to Hunger.

Of course, they didn't have to show up today like the rest of the class at the neighborhood school. At the children's service they prayed about we have done this and we have done that, we tattled, we hit, we spoke rudely. Forgive us, pardon us, grant us atonement. After the stained-glass windows darkened, they clamored over to Nanny's.

"You sure can cook, Miss Corinne," says Auntie. "I wish I could learn to cook."

"I 'member you making cream cheese just fine," says Miss Corinne. "'Fore Mr. Byron got his fighting uniform to save you peoples across the ocean."

Auntie had let the milk sour and brought it outside in a round metal container with holes in the bottom and sides so the liquid would drip through. What was left was Creole cream cheese, and with the right timing, the texture was of very thick sour cream and slightly more tart. That was about the time the letters stopped, asking for money to escape the Old Country.

Now a heavy roar of light and electricity cuts off the brightness from the glass chandelier. Tonight a cold front will come through.

Miss Corinne takes a pinch of salt and throws it over her left shoulder. The crystal salt shaker floats from hand to hand.

The little girl's brother yanks her pigtails, so she shouts, "Brother can't have *d'auberge* tonight." The tray of French *d'auberge* petit fours, small frosted and decorated teacakes cut in squares with eight alternating layers of chocolate cake and chocolate icing, waits on top of the icebox.

— *Cindy Lou Levee*

6:03 P.M.

As THE LIGHT FADES, a freight locomotive passes on a nearby track and blows its horn, prompting a loud burst of chirping in the cemetery's trees. Warren Kelly's red Ford Ranger pickup is always parked here, on the unpaved road that curves through Holt Cemetery, in the Lakeview neighborhood of New Orleans. The graveyard opened in 1879 as a burial ground for the "indigent dead." Today its massive live oaks and zigzagged rows of mounded graves sit behind a busy college parking lot, barely noticed.

Mr. Warren is a self-described "hustle man," a grave-cleaning free-lancer who earned his first money here half a century ago, as a teenager living in the Calliope housing project. Propped on his truck's open tailgate is a handmade sign: "Year round grave cleaning, painting & box building, headboards, adding of sand, upkeeping, etc. Call Warren beep 213-3123."

He wipes his forehead, cracks open a sixteen-ounce Natural Light, and looks in his rearview mirror, where two gravediggers in muddy boots dig a typical Holt grave: two and a half feet wide, six feet long, and about as deep as a gravedigger's waist is high. Sometimes their shovels pick up crawfish. At six feet down, they would hit water. Moisture heightens the graveyard soil's unique odor, the result of embalming fluid mixing with the dirt. Around new coffins the earth is often wet with beer or wine—friends giving the deceased a last drink. In the old days, people tossed in brooches or medallions, but that's rarely done anymore.

A typical family plot here holds dozens of family members, all buried in the same standard-sized grave, separated only by years. Each plot contains bones, because bones never go away. Any remains are deposited in a shallow hole right below the new casket. In New Orleans' famous aboveground tombs, a human body will deteriorate within a year. Down here in the soil it takes about six years. Anything less than that calls for a long iron tool known as a stiff hook. "Freddy Krueger ain't got nothing on what we see," says one gravedigger with a grimace.

Earlier, acorns crunched underfoot as mourners in black emerged from cars and trailed pallbearers with white gloves carrying twenty-eight-year-old Latoya McGary's light-blue casket toward an empty grave. Mr. Warren read about it in the newspaper. Her life was cut short by a gunshot to the head, he says. About twenty years ago, McGary's mother was stabbed to death and buried here in the family gravesite, also the final resting place for both her grandparents and her great-grandparents.

"They call this the potter's field," says Mr. Warren, re-telling the biblical story in which Judas, after betraying Christ, threw thirty pieces of silver onto the temple floor. Priests used that silver to buy land from the potter to bury the poor.

A few rows down, Mr. Warren's shovel stands idle, propped against a wooden marker. Without his care, that marker would rot away and this family's plot would disappear into weeds. That's what happened to plot C-623 after cornet player Buddy Bolden was buried there in 1931. A few years ago, a big stone Bolden monument was plunked onto unclaimed ground, but no one knows where he was actually laid to rest.

The gravediggers depart with a wave to Mr. Warren. His beer break over, he begins hoeing around a fellow veteran's grave. He was drafted for Vietnam, he says, right out of high school. There, he learned that sleeping on top of the mounded graves would keep him dry, even if the water level rose during the night.

Soon night will fall and, as usual, he'll be alone in the graveyard. Mr. Warren doesn't mind. "Dead people can't do you no harm, baby," he says. "You got to watch the ones that's alive."

— *Katy Reckdahl*

6:05 P.M.

IN THE COURTYARD OF YAWNING, dusk leans over the balcony falling and holding on like a drunk girl stumbling down the street.

In the slave quarter, she feels his fingers graze her beignet powder sugar thighs. Turns in bed to face him. He's not there. Never was.

Woozy stillness. Close, wet, hot. A sweat-bead snail inches down her spine.

On the river, fog horns and calliopes like barges collide.

The stereo's red light glows, comfort and crazy across the floor. Line dances on the rug, what's left of the sun. WWOZ on the radio dial. Old Babe Stovall moans.

Darker now, the courtyard. Fingers of fern poking between bricks, a Boo Radley house of broken windows next door; no one goes or comes.

She coughs uncertainly; the moldy walls.

Feels her pulse in her arm over her eyes.

Babe Stovall sings those "Woman Blues" and "I'm Gwine to New Orleans."

— *Janis Turk*

6:13 P.M.

SLEEK SAILBOATS AND SMALL MOTORBOATS PULL UP to the weathered dock, their occupants arriving just in time for a sunset dinner. Inside the busy restaurant, the bartender has all the work he can handle, and the waiters glide by as though they, too, are boats on the darkening river.

Families sit outside on picnic benches, cracking open crabs, peeling boiled shrimp, and talking loudly — about politics, sports, the conditions on the water. Loudest of all are two teenage boys. They cannot be a day over fifteen, and they are shouting, waving their hands in the air, and looking disdainful, as only adolescents can.

They do not argue about the local team, or cars, or even girls. They argue about how much tarragon should go into crab casserole. Their parents and aunts and uncles laugh at them. They could be in Tuscany or Paris, but they are not. They are in Madisonville, where the Tchefuncte flows, the seafood is plentiful, and Louisiana boys who have not yet begun to shave can brag and fight about cooking.

— Diane Elayne Dees

6:17 P.M.

"HOW IN THE HELL IS HE GONNA MANAGE THAT?" Justus asks, squinting in the dusk.

No one responds. Instead they all focus on the massive stack of barges that, until moments ago, had been laid up against the east bank a few hundred yards to the south of their campsite. Now, finally, as though the pilot's worked up enough gumption to try what appears to them an impossible feat, he has pried the whole apparatus away from the bank, which is why they've all six left the fire to stand at the edge of the bluff where they're set up. They want to see first-hand how he's going to move thirty-five barges, not just *up* the Mississippi, but around the ninety-degree bend to the northeast that they paddled through just hours ago. A nightmarish series of currents and eddies, the bend doubled the speed of their three canoes, forcing one pair of paddlers into the bank. Their boats, of course, only weigh a few hundred pounds each. The pilot, however, is going *against* those currents, and he's doing it with a few million tons of cargo.

Twain mythologized the river pilot, and rightly so. The job may be different today, but a pilot still must be able to navigate whatever cargo he is charged with, up or down this river, no matter the conditions. It's October now, so the sun's nearly down, its amber light filtering through the tops of the trees across the river. The guys wonder how he can see well enough to negotiate the turn. Twain said the pilot can see what he is doing with his eyes closed. They all wait. No one says a word.

As soon as the barges are in front of them, they can see how much water the tug's propellers must churn to make any headway at all, and the pilot's task becomes even more daunting. He edges by them, heading toward the bend.

"There he goes," Justus says, sensing it's all about to happen.

But he's wrong. The pilot stuns them all, shouting out, "Hey guys!" over a bullhorn. He sounds about fifty, with a scratchy voice that says he's given a few orders and had his fair share of whiskey. "Looks like y'all need some girls out there!" he calls out, his voice oddly cheerful in the twilight. He laughs over the tug's loudspeaker, and the campers huddled at the edge of the bluff join him in the revelry. He's the first pilot to ever hail them like this.

A moment later a deckhand steps out from the wheelhouse, and they, still laughing over the pilot, stop to watch him. He simply looks at them, turns, and moons them over the deck rail.

"What?" Doyle howls, and Guthrie laughs beer through his nose.

No one seems too shocked, though. After all, the crew on the tug is just a bunch of guys on a boat working the river; the ones on the bluff are just a bunch of guys who canoe a little piece of the river every year. The men on the river face unseen dangers and fight currents that engineers have been trying to tame for centuries; the ones on the bank merely fight their wives, friends and neighbors, and anyone else who hears about their annual trip: wives worry, friends and neighbors shake their heads, and a few people inevitably tell them, every year, that they will die.

The pilot aims the barges straight for the west bank of the river, about two hundred yards above where it bends sharply to the northeast. It's difficult to tell from where they are, but Vida swears the pilot touches the bank with the bow of the barges. Then, surprising them again, the pilot backs almost completely off the throttle. The river swings the tug, as silently and swiftly as a pendulum, toward the bank, and, at what seems like the last possible second, the pilot revs the engines again. Nothing happens at first, but soon he has her moving forward, sliding gracefully along the bank. Twain was dead on.

"Wow," Willie says.

The pilot disappears beyond the bend, sending a volley of whistles as he goes, and the guys head back to the fire they've made high above the river. Soon Brock will make his traditional pastalaya, they'll have a few beers, and they'll howl at the moon when it rises above the river tonight. Tomorrow they'll return to Baton Rouge, getting the same curious stares they always do as they pull their canoes onto the bank by the casinos.

— *Wes Dannreuther*

6:30 P.M.

THE OAKS' ROOTS GROW OUT OF THE EARTH like bent knuckles of a hand, fingers grasping the trunks. Dark green ivy covers the trunks and climbs up into graceful branches dripping with gray moss. The branches form a thick canopy protecting the earth below from Louisiana sun. At sunset, red, pink, orange, yellow, and blue light streams through the branches of the cathedral ceiling as it would through the stained-glass windows of a church. This natural filter makes it ten degrees cooler under the canopy, and St. Augustine is the only grass that will grow in the shade of the oaks. The ground beneath the fallen leaves is still damp from the last rainfall, and there is a musty smell from the undergrowth, yet honeysuckle vine's sweet scent overpowers it as it laces through the ivy. Finally, a hint of gardenia's heavy fragrance completes the moments spent here on this old front porch beneath the oaks.

Slowly, sounds from earth and trees come alive: birds singing, bees buzzing, squirrels playing, snakes and mice moving through the crackling leaves, insects humming, and acorns dropping to the ground from above. The oaks whisper.

On old maps, this place is called Live Oak Plantation, but the name is a bit pretentious for this humble house. On the porch, a grandmother tells her twin grandsons that their great-grandfather was a real cowboy and cattle rancher, and he taught their "G.G." how to ride horses under these trees. She reminds them of the scar on her forehead and tells them that the trees may still remember the day that a horse named Bertha kicked her in the head when she was two, and their great-great-grandfather who was a doctor made a house call to stitch her up just in time. The boys are four years old and can sit still long enough to listen to a story, even if it's about the chickens that once ran free on the porch of this little shotgun cabin where their grandmother once lived. The name of this town in Pointe Coupee Parish is "Poulailler," which means poultry house or chicken coop in French.

She points to the spot where their great-grandmother milked cows as a young bride, and they moo at the cows that are looking over the fence at them. She tells them to look high up into the branches, which once held the beautiful Japanese lanterns that lit up the night for a lawn party that her parents gave one evening long ago. When she tells them about the foundation of an old sugar mill on the property, the boys get excited and run into the yard to look for the same buried treasure that their father searched for as a boy. They begin to chase each other as they weave in and out and around the massive trunks of the old oaks. Eventually they come back to the porch and ask their G.G. to tell them more stories about a long time ago. She teaches them how to listen to the oaks from the old front porch where she sat with her own grandmother as a child.

Through the years volunteer baby live oaks have sprouted from the acorns that have fallen from the parent trees, and some have been used to plant other oak alleys. Others have been given as gifts to babies born in the parish as a symbol of a long and healthy life. A few of these trees grow side by side in pairs like old couples who have lived a long life together supporting each other while maintaining their individuality and dignity. Yet there is only one live oak alley here, where two rows of six great old oaks stand facing each other symmetrically like soldiers at attention waiting for royalty to arrive. The grandmother tells the boys that they are the royalty that the trees have been waiting for, and they smile with pride.

— Stacia Roberts Pangburn

6:32 P.M.

PAST THE JETTIES THE HORIZON BECOMES SCIENCE FICTION — an unbroken line of offshore oil platforms as far as Casey can see in either direction. Their dark metal frames rise like fortresses or battleships, looming over the Gulf waters. Lights twinkle. Helicopters move back and forth between the structures. Casey's fiancé is out there somewhere. He's a welder's apprentice; he's been offshore for forty-three days straight, working a double rotation.

Casey stands on the beach with her girlfriends, all of them perched against car doors, pulling from cigarettes, looking out at the waves. Silty brown water choked with pale clumps of seaweed. The boys sit just outside the breakers, bobbing on surfboards. They've been out all afternoon. Hurricane Emily is out there somewhere, heading for Mexico, pushing waves up onto the beach here at Port Fourchon. The boys like hurricanes. They sit on longboards between big jetties made from rock and broken concrete. That's where the sandbars push the waves into breakers. That's where they get good rides.

Casey can't get in the water because of her new tattoo. "It might get infected," she explains. The tattoo peeks out from behind her pink bikini top: a mermaid with a dagger.

"I wouldn't get in that water anyway," says one of her girlfriends, setting her beer down to adjust her ponytail. "That water's nasty. Whoa, look!"

Casey turns in time to see a bigger set of waves coming, marching toward the shore in long dark lines. The boys paddle hard, move themselves out into position. The first dark wall rises up, and the boy closest to the peak looks as though he's going to be swallowed up in the barreling water, but he pops to his feet, and the longboard glides down the slick brown surface of the water. He carves a turn at the bottom of the swell and rises again, flying along in the wave's curl. "Hiyaaaa!" he yells, wind carrying his voice.

The next wave is just the same. And the next. The boys balance on sleek fiberglass boards and angle toward the beach, laughing and calling, last ride of the day, until there is nothing left but white foam hissing toward the beach where it finally rolls up onto the sand. One by one, they step off in the shallows, lift their boards beneath their arms, climb out of the warm water. Casey watches their slick bodies as they laugh and run back to the cars, the girls, the music, the coolers full of beer and cold drinks. One looks over at her leaning against the hood of the car. "When are you going to let me see the rest of that tattoo, girl?" he says with a wink and a smile, saltwater dripping from his hair.

Casey hands him her beer, and looks out once more at the offshore platforms. Far away. Like clouds, sometimes they seem close enough to touch, and sometimes they seem so distant they might just cast off and disappear. She turns back to the cars, the drinks, the friends on the beach, all glowing in the long rays of afternoon sunshine. Things she can touch.

— David Parker, Jr.

6:36 P.M.

SOMEBODY TOLD HIM THERE IS GOLD IN LOUISIANA, and he believes it. Every weekend Marty loads up the old car with his gold-panning equipment, his rubber waders, a seventeen-dollar pan, a wooden fold-up camp stool he built himself, and his wife, Lanie. For months on end he drives into areas she has never heard of and she refers to as godforsaken, mosquito-infested swamps. But finally on this weekend, at this very minute, Lanie decides that maybe he is right, maybe there is gold here.

It started when a friend took out a tiny vial of water and showed Marty sparkling flakes of the stuff he had found settled in the bottom of Hemphill Creek. Tiny pieces the size of sand grains, but gold all the same. Marty joined the Central Louisiana chapter of the Gold Prospectors Association of America. He bought his first pan, a large, round, thick plastic pan with ridges on one side. The idea was to trap the heavier dark black sand in the pan and along with it the still heavier gold.

After weeks of Lanie watching him, sitting on the stool in bubbling little streams with sandy shores, where water ripples over fallen pines, digging the pan deep into the bottom of the creek, holding the ridged side in the water, all the while moving it in small circular motions allowing the finer top sand to escape, Marty announced to her, "I'm buying a dredging machine, because it can dig deeper than the pans. And the best part about it is the creek will fill the hole back up after we leave." She truly believed he had lost his mind, that he had developed "Gold Fever."

Now, months later the creek here cuts deep into steep clay banks lined with poles stuck into the wet mud awaiting elusive catfish. The dogwood and bright redbud bloom among the bare river willows and the grand, massive, weather-beaten oaks twisted and full of knots. The turtle doves whisper their secrets of true love. A flash of red through the trees and brush reveals a cardinal searching for his mate. And inside Marty's lungs embolisms are forming that will make this his last trip. Listening intently to the sound of the water tumbling over the small dam constructed by the hands of WPA workers long gone, Marty sits next to the dredging machine on his stool, in the middle of Little Barnes Creek, one hand holding small flecks of gold, the pan in the other, looking up at the golden sunset.

Lanie sits quietly beneath an old hickory tree absentmindedly fingering an agate he found on their previous trip, watching his contentment, and the gold in Louisiana.

— Anita Machek

7:15 P.M.

IT IS PAST SEVEN O'CLOCK and it's hard to find a place to park close to the funeral home, but that doesn't deter her. She maneuvers her big Buick into a space at the far end of the lot. As she slowly exits the vehicle and locks it, she makes a mental note to get there earlier next time. It just takes longer to do things these days. And sometimes the traffic in Church Point is heavy at this time of night.

She walks toward the main doors of the building, where several people, mostly men, are standing outside talking quietly. One holds the heavy door while another elderly gentleman greets her, *"Comment ça va, Madame Boudreaux?"*

She quickly responds, *"Mais, ça va. Merci,"* and without stopping to chat she enters the reception area, where more people are gathered. They acknowledge her arrival with a smile or a slight wave, but no one speaks as she makes her way to the crowded parlor, where the rosary has already begun.

The leader intones, *"Je vous salue, Marie, pleine de grâce, le Seigneur est avec vous. . . ."*

Soon strong voices throughout the room pick up the response, some in French, *"Sainte Marie, Mère de Dieu . . ."* Others answer in English or pray silently as they move their fingers deftly over the worn beads of their rosaries.

Mrs. Boudreaux finds a chair politely vacated by a young man and she sits. She removes her crystal rosary from its little crocheted pouch inside her purse and quickly tries to catch up. She notices her cousin is on the third decade and finds her own place in the ritual.

As she repeats the prayers taught her by French parents so very long ago, her mind drifts back to those days and other lost family members and friends. She scans the room to see those she knows and she finds herself making connections. Is that Gustave's grandson? Madeleine sure looks good after her knee surgery. Poor Josephine, her husband just died a month ago. Is that Allie's cousin, Rena? Was Nonc Robert's youngest son married to one of the

Richard sisters? Maybe Tante Marcelite's son was married to one? There's Madame Thibodeaux, such a kind and sweet lady, and spry at her age. Was her brother Geracin my age or my brother Sosthenes'? She used to remember those things so well.

She has to remind herself to focus on the task at hand and comes back into the repetition of the words that are so familiar in her daily life. This is the prayer she says every evening before taking her little heart pill. Sometimes, in the winter especially, she says two rosaries. Truth be known, she would rather be outside in her flower beds, but when the weather is bad, praying is a good thing.

The rosary ends with a litany of incantations to the Blessed Virgin and the saints. Soon everyone makes the sign of the cross and puts their rosary away as the ladies of the honor guard begin to mingle with the family members who have approached the coffin. Newly arriving viewers kneel on the prie-dieu as others in the room begin to talk amongst themselves in small, quiet knots. Laughter erupts occasionally but respectfully subsides.

Mrs. Boudreaux puts away her rosary and turns to greet one of her remaining cousins sitting directly behind her. There are so few of them left these days. After talking a while they decide the last time they met was at her younger sister's funeral last year. Has it already been a year? Where does time go?

— Evelyn Smith

To Peggy and Rick,
may this remind you of
Louisiana, of mommiee, and of
all of us —
With love,
Evelyn

7:38 P.M.

AFTER JOGGING ALONG THE LEVEE PATH down to the Florida Street pump station and back, he likes to stretch out at the end of the long dock in LaSalle's Landing and watch the sun go down. The dock is part of historic Rivertown in Kenner, and at about twenty feet high and some two hundred feet long, he can literally stand over the Mississippi River. More river at some times than others to be sure, and this evening the waters are drawn back about forty yards from the levee to reveal huge pieces of driftwood and other debris made by man and nature. Fishermen stand among it all on the river's edge, getting off a final few casts before the mosquitoes get too dense.

Anchored ships sit half a mile westward down the river, just far enough away that he can't make out the writing on the backs of their hulls in the dusk. Their deck and tower lights glow preternaturally bright, making their presence known to the line of airplanes on their final descent into Louis Armstrong International Airport. The river bends to the left further down from the ships, and the Luling Bridge becomes visible as the haze of the day burns off.

The only other people on the dock tonight are a young couple creating their own private, romantic moment. They've beaten the jogger to the best spot in the western corner of the landing. Warm breezes muffle their conversation as they lean deeply into one another. Her bare arm strokes his back through his untucked polo shirt. He tips a beer bottle back, finishing the contents much like a pelican gobbling its prey, and in a roundhouse motion hurtles the bottle over the railing. The smashing glass scatters gulls from their perches on the submerged debris of a metal dock below.

A white egret speeds along the river surface in sleek contrast to the awkward arc and splash of jumping fish. The jogger stares a hole in the back of the couple, but ultimately he says nothing. They all just continue to watch the sun drop, its deep red hue promising another sweltering day.

— *Chris Lenois*

7:41P.M.

EARLY JUNE TWILIGHT IN HOUMA means the time between sweet diversion and bed to ten-year-old Milo Sump. They have just finished a cold supper. Little Sister is singing softly to her doll baby on the front-porch steps of his small wood-framed house, and Mamma is busy putting "the *real* baby" to bed as he hurries to the J. E. B. Stuart Day School playground. He knows that when the cicadas sing he'd better be home. He can always find his way back by following the crosshairs of his mamma's yellow bug light and his maw maw's faint night-light. Maw Maw is bedridden in the back of the now-defunct store and tended to by a lady who sits with her in the day and turns on the night-light when she leaves.

Milo "strows" with purpose, the new oyster-shell road hurting his bare feet. He *has to* get to the swings—"The Bet" is coming (as it has for the last few years) and he must be ready this time. His mamma must have known too 'cause she let him go without a word, knowing full well that his cousin Jimmy will soon challenge him again this year—"Betcha can't get to the Magnolia Line 'fore I count to a hunnred."

There in the schoolyard stand the swings like silent tree vines. The bet is that if he can swing high enough to smell where the magnolia flowers are, by the count of a hundred, he will be big enough to play Tarzan by the swimming hole with the big kids this summer.

He picks his swing carefully, scooches his bottom on the wooden seat, and minces his way backward. Gripping the iron chains he pushes off. "No fair until I git started!" he yells to no one in particular, and as Milo pushes off he grunts with that first effort to become airborne.

He counts to himself as he has practiced the whole school year. He counts as Jimmy would, with the precision of an announcer at a rocket firing, only going up in the count instead of down.

"One, two, three, four," straining for flight. "Eight, nine, ten," beginning to get altitude. At the count of seventeen he bends to his work in earnest, working his body like a jackknife going up, tightening like a wrecking ball to achieve speed on the descent.

Up and down to the count, thirty-five, thirty-six, getting higher; he can feel the breeze on his scalp as he creates it, the sweat now drying as fast as it accumulates. Down like a meteorite, up and up like a steel spike being driven into the skies. He remembers his maw maw clutching his hand saying, "I've been a Christian all my life and now I'm afraid of dying."

Fifty-four, fifty-five, fifty-six, dropping like a ten-ton sledgehammer, curled into a ball, hitting the heights behind only to jerk his body into swimmer-precision straightness for the forward thrust, straining, pulling with all his might in the wooden chair on chains that will set him free. Up he goes up like an arrow, down like a shooting star. Pa told him this morning when they let him off at the ferry that goes into New Orleans, "Ah ain't gettin' back from this boat trip till near school time; you gonna haf to be the man now."

Eighty-five, eighty-six; the deal is "not the magnolias that you could reach from the ground or even the ones that you could get for your mamma or that pretty new teacher by standing on shoulders." No. "The *real* ones, the ones so high that only angels can pick 'em."

Ninety-two, wind whistling, the steady grunt of the pull, the hissing breath at the descent. Up like a shot, down like a rock. Up there . . . *pull!* Down there . . . *tuck!* Faster than an insult, ninety-four, ninety-five, falling like a gauntlet . . . and then . . . like the first breath after diving deep, with the setting sun as his witness, in his own created air stream, like a kiss from heaven comes the scent of the Magnolia Line. High up in the trees, almost into infinity he smells the citrus honeysuckle that is the taste of everlasting acceptance; and he rides until the chains jerk in his hands at the boundaries of what the swing can do, thinking himself at last worthy of reaching for the sky.

— *Phil LaMancusa*

7:48 P.M.

AFTER THE SUN FALLS BELOW THE BOULEVARD, an old truck turns off and rattles up to the house. Flo is out on the lawn, jumping up and down and waving. In the front cab Little Wilhelmena sits in shorts and a button-up blouse between Aria and Timbo. She scoots out soon as Timbo opens the door.

A happy jazz tune plays from the radio and floats over the prickly grass. Wilhelmena and Flo laugh and run like seagulls flying on a band of wind, the ribbons in their hair like little tails. They race to the very back and scurry up the furry-leaved fig tree, up the thick twisted limbs. Ripe purple figs are on the very top of the tree. The birds pecked the fat purple figs early in the morning. Those purple ones are the sweetest, ready to rinse and eat with milk. They don't need any sugar. The branches spread wide and far, creak-creaking, and Wilhelmena, being the smallest, balances on the thinner limbs.

Timbo saunters up to the pecan with a tin gasoline container, and Aria, right behind him in a yellow scarf, carries two broomsticks with rags on the ends. Aria hands Timbo a broomstick. Timbo tilts the tin container and pours gasoline over the wrapped rags. The roses on the sides of the yard glow purple in the twilight. Timbo lights a match in front of his face, and he shines behind the spark as the torches burst into bright hot flames.

Like Mardi Gras flambeau carriers twirling their fire, Aria and Timbo wave the burning torches to the tall, old pecan. The broomsticks stab at the silky worms' nests.

The girls climb higher in the green fig forest. The fuzzy leaves, soft and scratchy, brush their necks and cheeks; the sap and twigs drool and scratch their arms. Covered with sweat, they can't quit climbing.

The torches hit bull's-eye after bull's-eye; the bags of silky dust explode into flames. Silky webs tumble in a cluster and their song ends. Webs lie ripped and torn at the bottom of the pecan's trunk. Pecan shells fall to the ground, burning into bits. These pecans are rotten. Worms have already gotten to them.

Timbo reaches for the highest nests. "Theah we go," he whispers under his breath. Bright light of fire shines over the yard like the sun.

The girls are careful. Wilhelmena can stand on the highest branches. They reach out and pick some good purple figs.

— *Cindy Lou Levee*

8:00 P.M.

I WAS SEVEN YEARS OLD in June of 1954 when my dad and I drove from Miami to New Orleans to visit his friend Albert Thibodeaux. It was a cloudy, humid morning when we rolled into town in my dad's powder-blue Cadillac. The river smell mixed with malt from the Jax brewery and the smoke from my dad's chain of Lucky Strikes to give the air an odor of toasted heat. We parked the car by Jackson Square and walked over a block to Tujague's bar to meet Albert. "It feels like it's going to rain," I said to Dad. "It always feels like this in New Orleans," he said.

Albert Thibodeaux was a gambler. In the evenings he presided over cockfight and pit-bull matches across the river in Gretna or Algiers but during the day he hung out at Tujague's on Decatur Street with the railroad men and phony artists from the Quarter. He and my dad knew each other from the old days in Cuba, which I knew nothing about except that they'd both lived at the Nacional in Havana.

According to Nanny, my mother's mother, my dad didn't even speak to me until I was five years old. He apparently didn't consider a child capable of understanding him or a friendship worth cultivating until that age and he may have been correct in his judgment. I certainly never felt deprived as a result of this policy. If my grandmother hadn't told me about it I would have never known the difference. I once asked Dummy Fish, a friend of his from New York, if my dad had a job. "He talks to people," Dummy told me. "Your dad is a great talker."

Albert was a short, fat man with a handlebar mustache. He looked like a Maxwell Street organ-grinder without the organ or the monkey. He and my dad drank Irish whiskey from ten in the morning until lunchtime, which was around one-thirty, when they sent me down to the Central Grocery on Decatur or to Johnny's on St. Louis Street for muffalettas. I brought back three of them but Albert and Dad didn't eat theirs. They just talked and once in a while

Albert went into the back to make a phone call. They got along just fine and about once an hour Albert would ask if I wanted something, like a Barq's or a Delaware Punch, and Dad would rub my shoulder and say to Albert, "He's a real piece of meat, this boy." Then Albert would grin so that his mustache covered the front of his nose and say, "He is, Rudy. You won't want to worry about him."

Dad and Albert talked right past lunchtime and I must have fallen asleep on the bar because when I woke up it was dark out and I was in the backseat of the car. It was 8:00 p.m. We were driving across the Huey P. Long Bridge and a freight train was running along the tracks over our heads. "How about some Italian oysters, son?" my dad asked. "We'll stop up here in Houma and get some cold beer and dinner." We were cruising in the passing lane in the powder-blue Caddy over the big brown river. Through the bridge railings I watched the barge lights twinkle as they inched ahead through the water.

— Barry Gifford

8:12 P.M.

FOUR PROJECT PRINCES IN LARGE WHITE T-SHIRTS penetrate Nick's Original Big Train Bar. An old couple from the neighborhood grips sixteen ounces of vodka and shuffles to the door.

"Thanks for the fried chicken, Miss Louise."

"Four underwatas. Light ice. To go."

"It was delicious."

The old lady waves her free hand. The old man says, "All right, all right."

Jukebox tears swallow the air with melancholy, but no one seems to notice.

Jam-band hopefuls gather around the pool table with dirty hair and dollar Dixies.

Sheriff deputies watch the shiny lips of sorority girls move with verve, as the lovers lean into each other and away from their carnivorous dating past. The jukebox wails *hallelujah hallelujah*.

A politician slurs but keeps on clattering while a young woman feigns interest in her glass of wine.

A scream severs into the jukebox repentance. "Holy s---! It's snowing."

Heads snap toward the square glass panel in the slant of the door. "No way!"

A collage of colors tumbles over barstools, past cigarette embers held carelessly extended. They reach toward the battered door and push through.

Outside, flurries scatter beneath the harsh beam of a security light.

"Dude, that's not snow." Arms wave wildly.

"That's disgusting."

"Jeez, it's like eighty degrees out here." Bodies turn in retreat.

The little wood-framed shotgun turned barroom bows down in a wink. An off-duty bartender leans against the smudged white weatherboards that curve and dip like the wet sidewalk beneath his feet.

The city's finest waiters/musicians circle around their chosen mayor.

Beyond them, wardies fall out of thumping cars. Neighborhood people shout from their stoops to no one in particular. The door leading into the bar swings open and bounces closed, as college students flirt with desperation. The muffled jukebox squalls a last gasp of agony into the moist air.

"You know what I think?" The bartender calls his council to attention. He tilts his head up, lips pull tight, eyes expand, large and round and red. He takes a drag off his cigarette. Anticipation grows. He exhales. Sips his beer.

"I think—" His head bobbles. A stern gaze lands on a short little guy with dark-rimmed glasses. "I think Sal should get me another beer and that this is the most beautiful f---ing place I've ever seen."

Then he rushes forward and propels his beer bottle against the abandoned warehouse across the street. Glass explodes into glistening icicles.

Amid a forgotten clip of city, the immediate noise stops—

A siren sings in the distance. A prostitute sways down Tulane Avenue.

Beneath the light, termites swarm together a southern winter wonderland. A tribe totters forward to throw amber snowballs at a crumbling brick wall.

— Kelly Wilson

8:23 P.M.

A LITTLE WAYS DOWN THE BAYOU, in Chauvin, near "the end of the road" that gets closer each year, there's a blue house on stilts. In the backyard a family gathers to sing to an eighty-year-old man. His wife, mascara running partly from emotions, partly from heat, six grown kids around her, remembers the wedding. "I was fourteen and completely in love," she says before they sing. "I still am." Of course there is the smoke and smell of sausage, the jambalaya, the pecan cake. There are also thirty some-odd children in bright swim-suits, grand and great. Their running, wrestling, slip-sliding has paused for just this moment. One, a nine-year-old wrapped in a blue towel and blushing through her freckled tan, hides behind her father's arms while he laughs and she tries not to look at her moth-er singing on top of the picnic table. At the edge of the yard, where there would be a fence, a nephew and his lover balance on the roots of an oak and listen. Underneath the sounds of "Happy Birthday" is a different clatter, the sing-song belching of frogs from the slate-smooth bayou only five feet away. In a minute, when the sun finish-es disappearing, they won't be able to see where the ground stops and the water starts.

— Linda Rigamer

8:27 P.M.

SHE SLIDES HER PLAYER'S CARD IN and pulls the arm, though she doesn't have to, could just as easily push the button. But pulling the arm makes her feel like she's doing something, like she's in control.

In those moments when the sevens and cherries reflect off her bifocals, she holds her breath, watching her fortune tick by. No win. She draws in another breath, a combination of cigarette smoke and something clean and clear and pumped in from somewhere else. This is not the air just outside the door, air that smells like refineries and car exhaust and muddy lake water. No, this is the kind that makes you feel alive, the kind that someone pays for.

A redhead with heavy black eyeliner comes by and hands Millie a clear drink in a plastic cup—something with lime. "Here ya go, Miss Millie," she says and pauses for a tip.

Millie nods absently, not turning her eyes from the flashing lights, from Hal, who promises to make life sweeter some day. Hal is her favorite slot machine, a dollar slot, named after her late husband. "Hal's a lucky one. First time I won big it was right here." Millie stands up and stretches her legs. "The real Hal used to take me dancin'. We'd do the jitterbug and the Texas two-step. Died of cancer in '92." She pauses and sips her drink. "Guess the real Hal wasn't so lucky."

Last year alone, Millie claimed $14,000 in winnings to the IRS. Who knows how much she lost. There was no special booth to report losses. And besides, she says, she doesn't keep track of those.

Millie tilts her salt-and-pepper head back, peering from the bottom of her glasses. Up twenty-six dollars. She pulls on Hal's arm again. Lights blink and the Sirens sing their digital melodies from every direction, a sensory overload, but Millie blocks it out. The room melts away. She focuses on the machine's broad eyes, spinning around again and again. This is her night, and it's a good night for the two-step.

— Nancy Rowe

8:30 P.M.

THE DADDY READS TO HIS LITTLE GIRL of three as he customarily does in the evenings. She curls up in his lap and quietly listens and looks at the pictures. "Will you read me another one, Daddy?" "Yes, baby." He patiently reads book after book, never hurried. He cherishes this time with his child.

"Daddy, Daddy, will you play a game with me?" "Sure, honey." And they play a game of Go Fish. He loves to play games with his baby.

She asks, "Are we going fishing tomorrow, Daddy? Will you take me fishing?" "Yes, baby, I will take you fishing." In the morning they will head out to Cross Lake on the edge of Shreveport. They have a "secret hole" there where she always has good luck. Daddy will bait her hook and she will reel in catfish with her little Snoopy fishing rod. He loves spending the day on the lake teaching her.

As he tucks her into bed for the last time until her next visit the weekend after next, she looks up with big brown eyes and kisses her daddy goodnight. He reaches down, kisses her forehead, and tells her he loves her. Placing her little hands on his cheeks, she says, "I love you too, Daddy, and I want to keep you forever."

— Lina Hutches Beavers

8:42 P.M.

A TABLE OF TOURISTS SITTING AT NIGHT beneath the glowing rainbow of Pat O'Brien's courtyard fountain leaves their waiter two quarters for a tip. The waiter picks up one quarter and looks at it, then turns it around in his hand. He has on a clean white shirt, the characteristic green apron, sharply shined shoes, and a bow tie. He supports a large round tray in the flat of his left hand and turns the quarter over and over in his right. At a nearby table, two roustabouts from an oil rig and their girls laugh drunkenly, clash Hurricane glasses, and demand another round, but the waiter, absorbed in this quarter, ignores them. The tourists who tipped him watch silently. As he rolls the quarter between his fingers, others nearby pause mid-drink to look his way. When he has everyone's attention, looking to the sky, he grasps the quarter between his thumb and index finger and throws it straight down at the flagstones. Hitting square on its corrugated edge, the quarter makes a loud, flat "ding" and bounces straight back up to his hand. He catches it without emotion, slaps it back on the glass table, and walks off, not saying a word. The slap of that quarter still hangs in the air at Pat O'Brien's.

— Richard Louth

9:02 P.M.

"YOU GOIN' TO THE CHRISTIANS? I'm goin' to the Christians."

Brock says it to everyone he passes, making his way from Jackson Square along Decatur through the lower Quarter.

He asks his sleeping friend in the electric-powered wheelchair with his head slumped on a pile of clothes-filled plastic bags outside of Central Grocery, "You goin' to the Christians?" He pats him on the arm. He doesn't wake up. "I'm goin' to the Christians." Brock walks on.

"You goin' to the Christians?" he asks a gutter punk with an intricately tattooed face sitting outside a darkened Decatur storefront. The gutter punk doesn't answer but mockingly shakes his dog's muzzle upward. "I'm goin' to the Christians."

He passes a Dickies-clad hipster walking slowly toward Molly's and asks, "You goin' to the Christians?" No response. "I'm goin' to the Christians."

"The Christians" he's going to are an evangelical religious group that serves food to the homeless at 9:00 nightly at the riverside train tracks by the Governor Nicholls Street Wharf on the far edge of the Quarter.

When he gets there a hundred or so homeless and transient New Orleanians will work through the food line, gobbling up red beans or pasta or stewed chicken, downing it with bottled water and cans of Big Shot cola.

Someone will look up from his Styrofoam plate of Christian food and ask why they chose *that* place. Someone always asks that. And with good reason—between the empty train tracks and the big lonely wharf above it, there's no more desolate-looking place in the city than this vacant lot. Especially this time in January, when that fake-looking winter fog hangs lonesomely over all of them, undulating with the warm, briny breeze coming off the river, slowly shifting, rising, falling, and swirling lazily in ghostlike tendrils.

Someone will start a fight. A thoughtless jab for cutting in line or for no reason at all. But one of the Christians will pull the serving spoon behind her back and say something like "Be nice or be hungry" and the scuffle will break up pretty quick.

Someone will ask why they do it and someone will answer, "Don't ask why." Someone else will say, "It's cuz them Christians know when we get ourselves right and have a job and a woman and some kids we'll take 'em to church ev'ry Sundy—I know I will."

Out of respect for the Christians, Brock will try and keep the bottle of Old Crow from poking out of his pocket. He'll stay quiet on the line and he'll eat his plate of food. Then he'll head back to his bench in Jackson Square and try to stay awake so the police don't take him in for sleeping in public.

But on the short walk to the Christians, he's not shy and he's not quiet as he tries to round up whomever he can. "You goin' to the Christians?" he asks the guitar player on the corner of St. Philip and Decatur.

"Nine o'clock already?!" the guitar player cries, stopping in mid-song to jump up and pack his case and gear.

"Yup. Let's go to the Christians."

They hurry down the block together toward the Christian food line, passing the statue of Joan of Arc, which rises triumphantly into the low-lying fog, looking as tall as Manhattan's skyscrapers poking into that milky haze.

"We're goin' to the Christians!"

— Andrew Travers

9:16 P.M.

MAW MAW'S SHADOW DANCES ACROSS THE WALL as she goes from room to room lighting oil lamps while dusk turns to dark. The braid that had been coiled into a tight knot at the nape of her neck now hangs freely like a shining silver rope down her back and falls across her shoulder as she bends to offer a goodnight kiss. Mosquito netting draped around the antique bed sways gently in the cool winter breeze that whistles through the slightly opened window, and the final licks of flame shrink as the fire calms itself for the night. Silent prayers of thanks are interrupted by the cadence of croaking frogs, the mournful howl of an unknown animal, and the hushed voices of Maw Maw and Paw Paw as they sit waiting for the embers to fade to ashes. Sleep comes quickly to the child beneath the stack of handmade quilts, who knows she will soon be awakened by the smell of sweet, hickory bacon and the sound of it sizzling in Maw Maw's favorite little black skillet. Warm bread fresh from the oven will be covered with thick black syrup that pours so very slowly from the bright yellow can, its sweetness tempered by the bitter pureness of milk straight from the cow. This is a place and time of simple goodness.

— *Eileen Decoteau*

9:32 P.M.

THROUGH THE THICK AIR AT DUSK a dark pickup drives in. In the back is a johnboat, a shallow craft flattened on both ends. The driver, a thin graying man with a battered porkpie hat, says, "Name's Marvin Haney. I'm your gator man. These here're my assistants." He points toward the two plus-sized women in spandex shorts who step onto the running boards on either side of the truck. Once they launch the boat with its silent trolling motor, he directs a blue searchlight into the weeds. They inch along its eerie shaft toward the golden eyes of the mesmerized alligator. A shot thwaps out from Haney's crossbow, and an arrow with a line attached penetrates where the base of the gator's skull joins its broad back. As the three hunters reel it in, it tries to stun the boat with its thrashing tail.

They drag it into the cove. Elizabeth grabs David by the elbow. "Don't you go over there, you little dope." One woman keeps the line taut while Haney scrapes his oar through the smelly tangle of ropy vines around the gator's legs. It snaps down on the oar blade. At that moment the other woman swoops in and presses hard on its nose. The jaws cannot open against her straightened elbow. The woman herself has kept every hair in her bottle-blond coif in place. Mr. Haney takes over while the women stretch rubber bands over the gator's snout—the same fat blue bands you see in the produce department around broccoli stems. Then the blond straddles the gator, raises its head, hums tunelessly, and caresses the mosaic of tiny white tiles under its throat. "It's real soft here under the neck," she says to David. David may not remember much of this Louisiana Pietà, but his parents, sister, and grandmother are transfixed by blue light. One by one they bend down and stroke the smooth, pliant skin.

— *George Newtown*

9:33 P.M.

IN AN AIRLINER CROSSING THE ATLANTIC in the middle of the night, a flight attendant walks into the cockpit and says, "Aren't one of you guys from New Orleans?"

The captain smiles and raises his hand. "Guilty."

"There is some famous New Orleans band in business class. Check it out." She hands him the passenger manifest.

He reads it and nods. "Not just a famous band; the leader is from one of the New Orleans first families of music."

The copilot, fresh from a nap, decides to become the grammar police and asks how can there be more than one first family of anything.

"I guess you'd have to be from New Orleans to understand," the captain replies. "I'm going to stretch my legs—back in a few minutes."

He stops at the galley located just outside the cockpit door and pours a cup of Community Coffee. He brings his own supply on flights.

He walks up to the leader of the band and says, "Mister Marsalis, I thought you'd like to know there was a New Orleans boy flying you across the pond tonight."

A grin crosses Wynton's face. "Man, you didn't have to say that. 'New Orleans' came out as soon as you opened your mouth."

They start an animated discussion of items critical to New Orleans life. The Saints had won two pre-season games in a row. Would it be premature to make hotel reservations for the Super Bowl? Since high school rather than race or religion is the determining "root factor" in New Orleans, they debate the relative merits of high school football teams and marching bands. An agreement is reached that St. Aug's Purple Knights have the best marching band in the city for sure and perhaps the world.

The captain asks if they are playing a few gigs in Europe or going on a tour.

"Another tour," Wynton answers. "We have more musical talent in the city than the city can support; got to tour to make money."

The pilot nods. "Man, is that right! The other night my wife and I were having coffee and beignets at Café du Monde. There was this sound—it was a sax, but a sax like no other I have ever heard. We followed the sound up the Moonwalk to the river. The fog on the river was so thick you could hear the ships passing but couldn't see them. This old man was sitting on a box with a sax. I can't say he was playing a sax—it was way past that."

Wynton laughed. "That's Mister Tony. He lives down the street from me; can make a horn moan like a woman—just never got a break."

One of the other musicians interrupts and says, "Dude, I'm getting tired of all this New Orleans bulls---."

Wynton playfully slaps the man with a magazine and says, "If you ain't from there, you can't understand."

— Jack Saux

10:05 P.M.

THE PASSING PARADE OF BOURBON STREET is a precious mix of visitors, workers, hustlers, tap dancers, and barkers who can wheedle tips out of you, while charming and spiriting you into the clubs, often with only a wisecrack or two. "The more you drink, the better I look," says the guy with missing teeth. Regulars can discern the mood of the crowd in a few moments. Are they free-spending conventioneers on a junket, loosed from the meetings of the day, or are they romantic couples, arm-in-arm, wide-eyed at the spectacle swirling around them? Which direction are they carrying their drinks? If they're moving downriver, carrying mostly full cups, they're here to explore, stopping in a variety of venues, and staying as long as they're entertained, until the wee hours. If they're scurrying upriver, they've fulfilled an obligatory perusal of what they had pre-judged was too scandalous to share with the neighbors back home. Shocking: eight blocks of people drinking in the street, and Lord knows what's going on in those strip joints.

She sits in the door of the strip club, four steps up, for an hour before each show, attempting to fill the room by making eye contact and smiling broadly, hinting at possible debauchery inside. It's a Saturday night, overcast, but not too chilly. Perfect for her to display deep cleavage, flexing her breasts, which is what really calls for attention, despite her beautiful eyes.

Her long sparkly gown, teased hair, and war paint set the tone. We see a delicate choreography between the doorman barking, "Step right up," and her provocative demeanor. She makes her "cupcakes" bounce incessantly, feigning an innocent expression in reaction to the surprise on people's faces. Caughtcha lookin'—if she's so entertaining in the door, imagine yourself up close and personal, behind the door. When a couple passes, the stripper looks into the eyes of the woman, signaling to send her man up the steps, if only for a moment.

"Honey, why don't you do that?" the guy asks, staring at the staccato rhythm of the stripper's flexing breasts and trying to mimic the motion by shrugging his shoulders up and down.

"Teach me how you do that," the wife beseeches.

The stripper presses her hands together, shoulders down, elbows raised. "I must, I must, I must increase my bust," she lilts. The Middle America wife pushes her husband forward. The stripper points to her chest and draws his nose to her cleavage, leaving her mark. She pantomimes to the crowd watching from the street . . . *shhh*. Don't let him know there's bright red, waxy lips imprinted near the top of his balding pate. The wife is in on the secret, knowing that he probably won't find out until he sees his reflection. Laughing, they go inside. The crowd cheers. Temporary victory. The beat cops can tell how good a night the stripper is having by the passing numbers of bald guys with lip prints planted on their heads.

– GiO

10:16 P.M.

BOURBON STREET, WHERE IT INTERSECTS ORLEANS. Three hot young cops lean against their squad car. The cop in the middle is the Alpha cop, a gorgeous, muscle-bound, gym-toned specimen of bayou bad boy. He's wearing his short-sleeved uniform tight, tribal tattoo snaking 'round his bicep, flanked by his brother cops.

"And then," as stories and myths and legends and the real and absolute truth have it . . . "So it began, once upon a time, thus it was, and then . . ." And then a tribe of lithe women clad in shards of fabric clinging to curves in the semi-tropical wet heat of the night surrounds the cops. Like hummingbirds, the women tease and flit and sway to the zydeco, jazz, rap — the rhythmic cacophony that spills, jams, rams out of the open bar doors. The women come up; they pull back. They skit and flit and flirt about. The cops maintain their position, backs to the car, arms akimbo. One beautiful woman, a golden-haired nymphet, dark red lipstick staining the swollen pod of her mouth, kohl-rimmed eyes glistening, balancing on the pedestal of stiletto sandals, backs against the Alpha cop, joining up against him like wisteria to a brick wall, and she's that pretty, that fresh, that firm-yet-soft. She moves her hips rhythmically against him, pelvis go-go-going, dry humping him, the statue of Touchdown Jesus at the end of the block. And Jesus is still as a statue. And the cop is as still as Jesus. He stands with his back to the car and his front to the vision in tight jeans hootchie-mama-ing for him, book-ended by his brother cops. Heat and moisture. Life-lust-love become liquescence on a summer night in New Orleans.

The street and bricks, the parked cars, bodies and souls — all return the memory of residual heat. The cop reaches out two fingers, like an epicurean examining a piece of fruit, and delicately pulls back the waistband of the beauty's low-slung jeans and peers down into the mystery, the streetlight limning the scene.

— *Marci "Merci" Davis*

10:35 P.M.

SHE IS MIRED IN THE EVERYDAY TASKS of any night, scraping crumbs from a plate into the trashcan, placing dishes in the washer. The white-on-chocolate cake was a leftover from the gathering the night before — three struggling to learn to play bridge at the dining room table, and a fourth sipping wine as he taught. But now the table is where her husband, an engineer with the Army Corps, grumbles over the dimensions of a new levee. The baby, finally quiet after crying through a loud and sudden spring storm, slumbers in the semi-dark of his lamp-lit room. She is tired, but feeling crumbs on the soles of her bare feet, she reaches for the broom.

And then it hits. The sound, so easily recognizable in afterthought, is a mystery at the moment. There's a quick *whatwasthat?* and a mad dash to the front of the house, where a sheet of water glazes the foyer floor.

Open the door, she thinks. *No, wait, don't.* She looks out the front window. What was once a street is now a river. Slowly, a car eases past. Water ripples through the yard and up the driveway. She can hear the resulting wave hit the door and rush through the foyer, beginning its all-night seep through the house.

She runs to the hall closet for beach towels. She can't help but notice that they still smell of sun and chlorine as she shoves them against the door. From somewhere in the house she hears her husband yell that *It won't do any good,* that *It's too late for towels.* Following the sound of his voice, the opened door that leads to the garage grabs her eye, and what she sees stops her dead: already, the garage has two inches of water. Items of no importance — a single sock, a scented dryer sheet, a dirt-crusted garden glove — float by in the shallow bath. Already, the box of Halloween decorations is soggy, the electric goblins and witches ruined. She unplugs the washer and dryer.

Her husband emerges with a pair of sawhorses, a saw, and a wooden post. Setting up in the kitchen, he begins to make blocks to raise the furniture. She looks through the cabinet and grabs cans of Heinz Tomato Paste, LeSueur Green Peas, and Campbell's Cream of Mushroom Soup. She slides these under the legs of the dining room table and chairs.

As he saws, splinters and specks hit the floor. She pictures her baby's bare feet. She picks up the broom from where it had fallen to the floor and sweeps the mess into the dustpan. But then the next wave hits. And she stops.

— Katheryn Krotzer Laborde

Editor's note: This submission was received on August 22, 2005, one week before Hurricane Katrina made landfall in Louisiana.

10:49 P.M.

LUKE IS WEARING A FADED YELLOW T-SHIRT with a picture of two nutria at a sock hop. The girl nutria has long eyelashes and a poodle skirt. Luke says he has only been wearing the shirt for a day, and it's already so dirty he needs a new one. Luke gets new clothes instead of washing his old ones, because he's homeless. Luke is also wearing two rosaries around his neck, along with a purple string of Mardi Gras beads, but he's Baptist, not Catholic. Luke used to sing in the church choir with his sister. He sings a song about Jesus while he drinks his beer. He has also got on denim shorts and sports sandals. His feet are pale white where the sandals straps cover them up. His toenails are long and yellow and cracked.

Luke is sixty years old. His face is burnt red because he sits by the river each day. He was married for thirty-four years, but the Lord saw fit to take her home in 1990. Luke used to go to AA meetings five nights a week. He got his ten-year chip. He got a lot of chips. He gets $700 a month from the government. He was in the army.

Luke knows all the good places to sleep. One is on Magazine Street. He knows where to get free meals. They even give him cake. One time he busted his head open and his brains were lying right next to him, and then they put them back in. He has had six brain operations. He was born in Charity Hospital. He is from Marrero.

Luke gets arrested sometimes. He says he "killed six niggers" because he got robbed by one of them. They beat the s--- out of him for twenty-nine cents. Luke used to brew his own beer. It was eighteen proof, and flames rose out of the top of the bottle whenever you took a whiff.

Luke goes to sleep at seven each evening. Luke says he has a perfect memory, but he doesn't remember my name when I ask.

— Missy Wilkinson

11:08 P.M.

DESPITE A MISHAP WITH THE FULL SODA in the cup holder and a small scrape on her back from the seatbelt fastener, the sex had been lusty and satisfying. Now, sitting in the middle of the bench seat of his truck in front of the radio, she faces him. His left arm drips over the steering wheel. She pulls her left knee up under her chin and glances at the clock to calculate how long it is until she is expected home. While tucked on the other side of the levee from Highway 23, hidden from the traffic of Belle Chasse Highway, the canals had exhaled brume during their lovemaking and submerged them. He waves his hand out of the window, as if gesturing someone to pass them, and comments, "Pa's out steering in this tonight. Been hangin' out down in Pilottown all day waitin' on a Chinese freighter."

Using her thumbnail to scrape at his cuticles, she cleans each finger on his right hand of the oil residue left from his day of working at the refinery. He flinches and adds, "I guess we could've parked on the other side of the highway and watched for the river traffic."

"We wouldn't see nothin' in this anyway," she says as she wipes a line of grease from her nail onto the seat. "Not that we'd even know which one was his if we could."

The fog drills into his bones, and he quickly rolls the window up with a shiver. "Nights like this almost make me glad I lost that election."

Interrupting his manicure for a moment to scratch her nose, she shifts a little as she timidly responds, "Every night I'm glad you lost. I never thought that DUI would actually be worth somethin'."

"Pa said if I try again in a couple of years, let it blow over, I should get voted in. River pilots take care of their own, you know, they just gotta be careful. Pa and Uncle Forty both said it was real close last time." Silent, she continues her attention to his hands, scraping beneath his nails, caressing his calluses.

"You can't do it just for the money, baby. And look,

ConocoPhillips is giving you nights and weekends—you're not gonna get that piloting."

"I wouldn't say they're giving 'em to me. They're just not paying me to use 'em. Besides, what do I use them for anyway? Drinkin' beer? Hangin' out with you?"

He stares forward as if to admire the scenery outside the windshield, but there was nothing to study but impenetrable confusion and thickness. He doesn't understand nor protest when twenty-two minutes early she quietly sniffles, "Take me home."

— Julia Carey

11:32 P.M.

YOUR FRIEND LINDA DRANK TOO MUCH, and now they're giving her vitamins. You're stuck in the waiting room at Charity, while outside Endymion rolls. You dress sensibly — jeans, sturdy black boots, and your boyfriend's sweatshirt. Today you braid your hair and put on a pair of your best beads. You keep a camera and wallet in your front pocket. You like having free hands. And free hands came in handy when you propped up Linda from the neutral ground so that she wouldn't rest in her own vomit. Still, the paramedics insisted on moving her from the Mid-City festivities to the hospital.

"Where do you want us to take you, baby?" they asked.

"Charity," she muttered. "I have no insurance."

Since you were the odd woman out — your boyfriend stuck behind a bar on Bourbon Street — you rode up front in the ambulance and now you are here in Charity Hospital's waiting room among solemn faces, those praying for good news about gunshot wounds. You are the only one wearing Mardi Gras beads. You are too drunk to feel self-conscious but, fortunately, not nearly as drunk as Linda. You sipped slowly on beer, not a fifth of Southern Comfort.

Outside faint whoops and hollers of a party going on without you echo. The drums sound and you feel it in your chest. In the waiting room, there's no television, nothing to read, and, least of all, nothing good to drink, so you get up from your seat and mumble something about stretching your legs to the half-sleeping woman next to you.

You breathe in the outside air and suddenly you are wide awake. You follow the drums, find the parade, and push your way through the crowd. You missed Endymion earlier since the Mid-City crowd was too thick, and then there was Linda. Drunk Linda. Sick Linda. Now is your only chance to witness the fiberoptic snake that meanders through the city, to feel the horns' blast up close, to grab more beads.

"Hey, mister," you yell. The masked man won't throw anything for free. Linda felt no fear, no shame earlier when she practiced yoga moves outside a ghetto grocery store on Broad Street. She was not worried then and why should you be now? Spurred by the anonymity of the pack of people, you grip the bottom of your shirt and raise it up to your chin, making sure to lift your bra too. The masker nods in approval of your young breasts, nipples made hard by the night air, and tosses a strand of thick white and blue beads, medallions from the krewe. Satisfied, you turn back toward the hospital and wait for Linda to wake up.

— Sarah K. Inman

11:44 P.M.

THE VICODIN YOUR CO-WORKER GAVE YOU a half-hour ago is starting to take effect. You pull a tap on a fresh keg and hold a plastic cup under it to catch the initial spit of foam. When the beer runs clean, you hold a new cup underneath and make sure there are more within reach. You lean forward on the bar shelf, back to the crowd, still.

Beer sales have been simplified to accommodate the Bacchus Sunday rush. Twenty-one identical Miller Lite tap handles are spread out in front of you, stubby, blue, and in formation like the Union pieces on a Stratego game board. You sell only one size. Large.

You fill cups and place them on the counter in front of you, where they are immediately whisked away by the rest of your co-workers. You have spent three sixteen-hour shifts with these people, and they have become the only people you know. Somewhere on the other side of the bar, out in the world, you have friends. You even have a woman you live with and love. But they do not exist anymore as people. They are simply part of Them, the humanity that rolls in and out the doors in wave after wave. Crashing, receding, resurging.

The music is loud. It is a techno mix via digital cable radio. You can't distinguish any song except "Smack My Bitch Up," which has now rotated in. You are asked an obvious question from a co-worker behind you and you nod without turning. It hurts to talk. Something about the bass and the vibration of your vocal cords makes your fillings ache. The beer streams uninterrupted, your motion reduced to alternating which hand holds the cup underneath. Everyone around you is working frantically, but you are still and you face the bamboo-covered wall. You don't have to look at Them. You think about the commerce of what you are doing, how the price of one beer will pay for the hour you work pouring all the others. You and your co-workers are the cheapest expense in the overall cost of doing business. The sound system, the fluorescent lighting, the air conditioning, the Bourbon Street lease agreement. All are more valuable than you. If the owner had to choose between saving your life or the walk-in cooler where the kegs of beer you draw from are stacked and ready to be sold, he would choose the cooler.

Still, you are a conscientious worker. Each cup you fill has an attractive head of foam, but you do not crave a beer for yourself. You may be floating on painkillers, but you are not drunk. You do not want to be drunk. You do not want to be part of Them. They are no longer human beings. They are masses of flesh draped in various fabrics. They spray urine and money in every direction. You don't have to turn to look at them to see them. You've seen them before. You could turn an hour from now, two hours from now, and the picture will be the same. Subtle shifts in color and shape, maybe, but all part of the same oozing entity.

The keg you have been pouring from has kicked. You move six inches to your left and pull another tap.

— Joe Longo

11:52 P.M.

THE AIR'S NOT SUPPOSED TO FREEZE along the Mississippi, but it has, the swamp fat and river bloat gone icy despite the timber still chuffing red up top the levee. Santa will be glad they stacked logs like cabins, choo-choos, pyramids, and army tanks then torched them to guide him in, even though the shapes have long ago unshaped to heaps. He might be glad for the heat too. They sure are—Rob, Tom, and Huck—out meandering from Baton Rouge for hours like days, looking for levee fires to push away holiday gloom, a chill unnatural, and a desert war looming. They've been lost all night on back roads and sugarcane plains, finally crossing the Sunshine Bridge and winding on River Road from Donaldsonville toward St. Gabriel, laughing out wow at chemical-plant towers strung with lights rising from blackness, their brains lit too from Xmas booze and paper squares like little presents. Now they've found them. The fires. Their remnants at least.

Car angled into ditch, they step into the cold and let it grab their breaths. Above them, dark figures move like living shadows against bonfire's smoldering glow. Rob, Tom, and Huck toast the last of another six and smile before they make the hike up. Tom and Huck are nicknames only accidental to Twain, but the names apply; they long to see the river dark and touched by lighted barges, smell its story in their veins. Hoots come down to them, then bottle rockets tracing sparks bounce off their car. Loud laughter carries on the frozen dank. The trio shouts back and shuffles their feet on grass iced crunchy. Then a big boy breaks from the blackness, unshirted and glowing white, shoeless, sprinting parallel to the levee.

"Where you going?!" they shout.

"Wherever my feets takes me!" he says, and runs on.

Yes, they've wandered, beneath banners of "Joy, Joy, Joy" that set them to chanting, and into small town bars where even their pinwheeling eyes were correct in seeing knives in other eyes. Wandered a long time—Huck after his father, distant as a quasar and more elusive than any Christmas star; Rob since that old jungle war so fecund with blood and nightmare; Tom in pursuit of words for his mother gone this year. Here, though, they are found. The levee ramping before them. Drunk kin zipping fireworks down.

They laugh and shiver. "Onward and upward!" they say. And trudge the incline toward any warmth that's left.

— Tim Parrish

MIDNIGHT

IT IS MIDNIGHT AT CHARLIE'S BAR in the Irish Channel, the time every night the guy with the peg leg, known as "Peg Leg," goes out and shoots his gun at the sky. No one knows why he does this. Some say it's because he is a Vietnam vet. Tonight he hobbles out through the moonlight into a streetlight. His pants are stained with whiskey. He looks up at the sky and points the gun and shoots as he wavers back and forth. The Chihuahuas in the yard of the house next door bark but no one else seems to notice. Peg Leg goes back into Charlie's for another shot of whiskey.

— Minter Krotzer

12:03 A.M.

THE TWO HEAVY RED METAL RAMPS on the *Thomas Jefferson* are already rising from the ferry landing on the Canal Street side of the river as the young couple illegally runs down the rough metal grating of the car-loading entry. The pounding of their footsteps joins the metal-against-wet-metal creaking of the ramps as they race past the already lowered traffic arm, jump the swiveling I-beam barrier, and leap aboard the last ferry from the East Bank to Algiers. The ferry worker, wrapping his mammoth ropes as they land with a thud on the metal deck, shakes his head and walks to the steps that lead to the pedestrian seating area. He lights a cigarette as he sits down for the five-minute crossing. He cannot see that this crossing is imperative to them.

"We decided this was the right thing to do," the young man says to her as they regain their footing after the jump. "We made a pact and it can't wait till morning."

At twenty years old they aren't breaking a sweat although he, dressed in oh-so-retro polyester plaid pants, a brown deer-patterned ski sweater, and a very broad ship captain's cap topping his chin-length brown curls, is attired in a manner more befitting a Nor'easter than the warm mild breezes sweeping across the deck. As they cross the deck to the railing, she clutches something in her fuzzy purple scarf and he clutches her around the shoulders. Her knee-length black wool coat is tight across her back as she hunches over the scarf's contents protectively. She is wearing classic Decatur Street starving artist thrift-shop chic, including cropped bell-bottom pants on top of black and white Oz-striped stockings, and a very worried look.

He leans his Amish-bearded face down to her ear and whispers something through the tight knit cap that holds down her very short hair. She checks the contents of the scarf again, and he peers down into it with her. Without any further discussion they hold the scarf over the railing and open it. They watch with sorrow as a lifeless tiny brown sparrow falls out of the scarf and into the current. Having seen old movies of burials at sea in which the shrouded corpse, placed on a board and tilted off the deck of the ship, obediently sunk to the bottom of the ocean, she peers over the side of the ferry railing and expects to see the sparrow sink like a stone to the river's mysterious bottom. Instead, the creature's body remains on the surface, becoming smaller as the water shrinks the feathers to the skin. It swirls, caught first in the relentless current of the river and then in the wake of the ferry. The girl's eyes are wide and wildly hysterical as the ferry moves toward the Westbank and the tiny brown bulge on the Mississippi's surface sinks, surfaces, sinks again, and then is slammed by a tree being tossed toward the Gulf in the river's rage. She starts to cry and sinks to the deck in a squat, her Doc Martens appearing to be all that is holding her up in her grief. He sits beside her and wraps the now-empty fuzzy purple scarf around her neck to keep her warm and they wait to reach the other side.

— Sam Jasper

12:11 A.M.

I WENT TO NEW ORLEANS for a weekend once. And four years later I suddenly realized I hadn't been sober for more than the time I'd spent in jail and didn't have a cent either. It was time I got my life together so I married my sweetheart, a tattoo-covered five-foot-tall powder-keg who just happened to own my favourite bar. I know what true love is. And our reception at club 666 is still being talked about but that's another story.

We were so in love she dragged me from the party to the levee to sing me some southern love songs. Down through the fog, hanging moss, thick warm air, down to the black, inky, swirling waters of the mighty Mississippi.

She was dressed as a mermaid and I was a golden boll weevil so we looked fabulous when we both ran after hearing a big splash and found nothing but Aaron's Scarlet Pimpernel outfit lying on the bank!

Upon it lay this note, which I will read word for word, because they are Aaron's words, not mine.

Don't explain . . . not an apology, merely an explanation.

Pride gets in the way like breathing when I dive into the lake of fire that is my very heart at the heart of it all, beating and trembling. No longer able to fake a smile or any of the pleasantries of drink in the watering hole of thirsty sheep, smiling and shaking hands to the same worn out hip tunes that lose their meaning in the mundane decadence of last call when we mouth the right words but never try to understand each other. No, it's so much easier to pretend to be moved by my words than to listen to the sadness that fuels the fire for nothing more than your entertainment.

When I ceased to be the court jester-clown on a stage performing like the conductor's monkey for your applause or a freak lying on the sidewalk reciting a history too real for you to understand . . . that is, when I needed someone to understand me for a change, things became uncomfortable. I don't expect you to understand that it's the same fathomless pain that makes it possible for me to walk through life alone and take down the notes that make up the book you like to read (so long as the characters never get real enough or close enough). You go home and I go to stare at the sun rising above the river until my tears are dry and I no longer feel like jumping. Sorry if I offended you by wanting to dance, I just thought for a moment you might understand my need to be understood. . . . I guess I was wrong.

We sprinted back to our wedding party for help and found Princess God and Aaron dancing naked on the stage.

— Mick Vovers

The cops are here; you know them all, so it's not a problem. So long as it's an out-of-towner, you've got a pass. Another night on the bayou, and the frogs and garfish don't care what happens to you.

— Graham Clarke

3:12 A.M.

WHEN LES ASKS THE GUARD why Death Row is not air conditioned, the guard says, "Neither is hell. This is practice." Les is joking; he is pretty sure the guard is not.

It is always hot and damp on Death Row—or always cold and damp, depending on the season. Les's cell is in the middle of Tier A, a lower tier—one six-by-eight barred closet (with toilet) in a row of fifteen closets, seven rows, over ninety men, in one old building, living one more ordinary day in a stretch of 4,380 days (on average) before they will die on the lethal-injection table at Camp F.

If it was 3:12 p.m., the tier would be a near facsimile of hell—fiery hot and clanging with the noise of the TVs in the corridor, the men talking and playing chess through the bars, one man at a time out for exercise inside or out, the shower at the end of the hall. There is too much commotion, like being trapped in a tin can and someone beating the outside with a stick. Les sleeps through the heat and noise of the Angola daytime and stays awake all night.

He gets up after they shut off the TVs, writes letters, and reads magazines while he slowly eats his supper from the Styrofoam box the trusties leave at 4:00 p.m. He works out methodically—sit-ups, push-ups, lifting his footlocker and laundry bag loaded with books. He does his correspondence lessons from the English and philosophy courses he is taking from LSU (he does not expect to be alive for graduation, much less be present at commencement), and then reads.

At 3:00 a.m. he begins two thirty-minute periods of za-zen, sitting meditation. He pulls out the zafu cushion from his footlocker and sits in the half-lotus position on the floor of his cell, turning his back to the bars and facing his toilet. He puts his clock on the toilet seat, to make sure he does not lose track of time. This is his favorite time of day—the only good time of day—his religious experience. He is a Buddhist because it suits his view of the universe, and because it confounds all the fundamentalists trying to save his soul on Death Row.

It usually takes him about fifteen minutes in the first session to get completely into it. It is perfectly still on the tier, a breeze is circulating the damp air through the windows on the opposite wall, the lights—always on—are subdued enough not to glare. He is almost there.

Les's eyes are open. He is looking at a point through the cell wall. His hands are cupped in the oval mudra position. His body is still and quiet. He is counting the breath. Inhale, one. Exhale, two. Count to ten. Start over. Notice the thought. Count again. Notice the thought.

He is seeking that simplified space where he will be liberated from suffering—from his thoughts of the girl he killed, from the legal issues that have kept his case in court for ten years, from his "neighbors," the other killers around him and the guards assigned to control them, from the lawyers and the preachers and the members of his own family, from the big mess of his life, from the pain and death of this world.

Later the official day of Death Row will begin. Men will start waking up, going to the toilet, yelling, singing, crying, the trusties will bring the breakfast trays, the worldly noise will commence again. He will eat, visit with the others, take a shower, and go to bed in late morning after he watches CNN and the morning talk shows.

But this time is still hours away. He is lost in this minute . . . 3:12 a.m., the clock says. Counting, breathing, noticing, searching for enlightenment . . . that he may be liberated, and share its liberation with others. By his count, he has 543 days left to search. Already . . . and not yet.

— *Burk Foster*

3:39 A.M.

ROLLING TO A NEW SPOT on the wrinkled bed sheet, he kicks the damp cover off and presses the pillow against his face and torso and loins to soak up at least some of the sweat, then flips it beneath his head, reaching back to lightly grip the bed board. The weight of night heat lies evenly across his skin. He rolls his bald head from side to side, flips the pillow over to find the older, cooler sweat, then raises the "ears" of the pillow to dry his face again; nothing cool about living on an old bayou houseboat in summer.

Beyond the window above him, a sharp buzz of a million crickets fills the woodsy blackness with one long note. A beetle ricochets against the belly of screen.

He folds the pillow in half and reaches through the darkness for the wineglass on the side table. His hand always finds it deftly, even when he's half-asleep.

Something surfaces in the bayou, just beyond the gunnels. He listens as it swipes across the surface of the water, bumps against the bow. Gators are never shy about a meal. The houseboat toddles in the wake; a picture frame slaps gently and rhythmically against the far wall.

— Patrick Burke

3:50 A.M.

ARMAND STEPS OUT OF THE CAMPBOAT onto the frozen marsh grass of Point au Fer Island. He rubs eyes that will not close in sleep, although yesterday's long hours of running traps and hauling muskrat pelts had left him with aching back muscles and exhausted limbs.

Cold penetrates his old woolen jacket, but he takes in greedy sniffs of the loamy air. He decides he has been cooped up too long in the stuffy boat cabin crowded with snoring Père, quiet Mère, and his younger *frère,* Joseph.

The match he holds to his cigarette flares a brief hole in the darkness he does not fear. He looks up at the star-gorged sky, and although he can make out only the far-off tree line, his eyes scan the horizon.

"Feu-follet!" he speaks aloud, startling himself with the sound. There, many yards away, wisps of flame rise from the ground. He knows that Mère would cross herself and whisper in Cajun French, "The soul of an unbaptized child!"

The crunching of his few retreating footfalls jolts him back to reality. He snickers at his momentary lapse into superstition. He faces the flickering marsh gas, and admires the muted light show.

Armand turns back toward the campboat. Work begins at dawn.

— Claire Domangue Joller

4:23 A.M.

THE HOLE WAITS IN THE ROAD at the corner of Coliseum and Upperline in the Uptown neighborhood of New Orleans. It is small. It has been small before and it will be small again. But sometimes it is large: big enough to swallow a Winn-Dixie shopping cart or a baby stroller or the front end of a United Taxi. After the hole begins to devour these various conveyances, the men in jumpsuits arrive with their backhoes and dig at the hole. They fix the pipe, or so they think, and fill the hole with sand and gravel and pour hot asphalt on the hole and roll the black macadam tight with heavy machines. But the hole is patient. It can sense the water still seeping from the rusted black pipe below, eroding the sand and gravel and flushing away the cigarette butts and the discarded wrappers from the Rally's burgers that the work crews have left from previous repairs. First the hole eats its way under the asphalt, causing a mild depression. It can feel the cars jolting as they pass overhead. Then one day a small chunk of the pavement gives way and falls inward, and noon sunlight enters the hole and warms and softens the earth below. A neighbor places a flag or a traffic cone or a trashcan over the hole to warn off passing motorists. Once a beautiful woman placed a potted palm tree over the hole but a student from Tulane stole it in a matter of minutes. The hole feels the rumble of trucks from above loosening the joints of the water pipe and the water flows faster. The hole has been growing quietly below the street. The black surface is undermined and about to give way. The hole hears the newspaper delivery truck approaching and widens its maw in anticipation.

— Iain S. Baird

5:35 A.M.

GOLDEN MEADOW. The moon, white and slender, hangs the tip of its horn over the blinking neon sign of Pierre's Palmetto Motel. In the east, the sun is just showing its forehead. Still tufts of cordgrass and pickleweed line a narrow channel rolled out like tin foil, crimping at the edges and slicing through the marsh. The muddy, tangled tapestry of slender rushes bunch in dense profusion with bases of chalky butterscotch and stalks that rise in successive shades of chestnut, banana green, rouge, amber, gold, and finally bright ochre at their cylindrical seed heads. These wheatlike tips glisten in the nether time between night and day. Brackish water gently laps the smooth hulls of fishing boats. Crickets and frogs hum. A bird laughs low and heartily. Cluckings, clickings, whistles, and buzzings permeate the reeds. A fin suddenly pierces the surface of the water and flashes in a neon ribbon of light. Gulf winds ripple the water as the narrow edge of the sky turns warm and golden.

— *Veni Harlan*

6:02 A.M.

ON THE BIKE ON DUMAINE STREET under the gray canopy of the early morning and the silence lifting and dispersing like the fog, the bright white tomcat in the window of the hair salon with the tail dyed in Mardi Gras tiger stripes, the purple band at the tip fading and the cat bored and smug. Passing the industrial building of a man with his steel-wool beard and rubbery lips who leans against the sex-shop storefront, the glossy picture of Grandma on the gift bag giving the finger in the display behind him and the beefy man saying, "Mornin' baby." Crossing Decatur Street and on the other side the three-coat wino who lodges under the awning of the candy shop with his nimbus of dirty hair, the smell of piss and stale alcohol and chocolate drifting through incoherent whispers and the zigzag flutter of the pigeons high on beignet dust just shy of the bike's wheel. Rolling through the public parking lot with the scattered, comatose cars, up the brick ramp to the Moonwalk, to the wide crescent in the caramel gray river, the creamy foam on the banks below and the moldy breeze and the body odor of the young Goth bums knotted together on the grass that creeps down to the jutting rocks. A short, impatient foghorn blast from the ferry launching at Algiers Point, small in the distance like a hard used Tonka toy, building speed across the boiling water and barely growing to adult size amidst the mammoth tankers and steely freight haulers. The ferry pushing through the oily wind as the symmetrical bumps under the bike tire grow faster and faster, rolling past the stunted trees corralled in wooden boxes, past the boarded-up tourist information booth with red, limp graffiti declaring, *The Revolution Will Not Be Televised,* and past the homeless man with the crusty hands, the cracking, desert face, who occupies the last bench before the sharp *L* turn, the left turn that brings the floating barges of the Bollinger Shipyard across the Mississippi into view, its cranes and counterweights like far-off erector sets from childhood. And the man on the last bench before the turn, swallowed up by scarves upon coats upon shirts and thread bare, the man who always says, "Mornin' baby."

— *Susan M. Folkes*

6:20 A.M.

TALL DRY GRASS RUSTLES against the truck's undercarriage as the driver pulls to the side of the road to wait for others to climb up. Another family hurries down a dusty lane, afraid they might be left. A stand of pine trees filters the dawning sun, but yellow streaks of light arc into the eastern sky. The predawn chill has evaporated, and the Grant Parish day ahead promises to be seasonally hot.

It's 1938. Pruitt Caldwell has gotten his whole family jobs on a cotton-picking crew and promised each child could keep a portion of what he earned. The two youngest could have three cents a day for their very own, the middle one a nickel, the teenage boys, Wayne and Jeff, seven cents. All with cut squares of a tattered bed sheet fashioned into large white handkerchiefs and tied around their necks to protect them from relentless needles of the sun, the Caldwells wait standing up in the truck bed, jangly from bouncing over potholes and jostled from lurching starts and grinding stops to board families just like themselves.

Pruitt faces away from the family running toward the truck. He's a lumber man, goddammit. But with the mill closed, he has no choice but this. All the millable lumber in a forty-mile radius has been bought up, chopped down, sawed up, sold off, and hauled away. The company has opened a new mill in Jonesboro, but that's seventy miles away. He couldn't move his family there. The Caldwells have always lived in Grant, where his own six acres are, where his wife, Osby, keeps their garden and hen house and cow when they can afford it, which they can't anymore. Where their house is. The house they own, where Osby cans peaches and makes preserves to smear on cornbread squares and sweeten coffee.

No one's interested in Pruitt's land, which isn't bottomland and isn't good for anything other than a garden, only middling land for that. Osby's corn is always stunted, no matter how much manure she and daughter Vivien spread around it. Not that Pruitt would ever sell his land. That land is his, with his house on it. And Jonesboro is too far away to make it back and forth every day, even if his truck still worked. So Pruitt figures he's out of the lumber business until the trees grow back. When will that be? When his grandkids are pointing out his grave to their children.

So now this. Picking cotton. Work not fit for a white man. But now the only work there is. So he'd pick, and his wife and kids would pick until their hands were raw. But he'd walk in a second if they put even one of them into the field beside him. He told the crew boss that, and the man spit in the dirt and said he understood.

The driver races the truck's engine, and the hurrying family waves and hollers out. Pruitt stares across the road at a vast stump field just like everywhere now in central Louisiana. Where once stood a forest of live oak, bald cypress, and red maple, Pruitt now finds an ugly, snaggle-toothed wasteland, a devil's grin of blackened tree bottoms and a viperous protrusion of root intermingled with tangles of scrub brush and the occasional worthless scraggly pine, bowed and frail like an old man who's lost his cane, all of it shrouded in a veil of mist that drapes over the surviving vegetation like a spider web.

After the mill closed Pruitt went to a meeting in Alexandria where a man called the disappearance of the Louisiana hardwood forest a tragedy. He said cutover land was sad and hideous, an abomination. Said God's beauty was despoiled. Pruitt thought the man was a fool. The forest wasn't beautiful. It was work. Good work. White men's work.

Pruitt sneers at the stretch of cutover. The forest has always been there to provide raw material for his livelihood and should be there still. He mutters a curse upon the forest for disappearing, the forest itself that has disappeared and chopped him down to the level of a field hand.

The new family finally scrambles aboard; the truck jerks into motion and gathers speed. In contempt for the cutover, Pruitt spits at the stump field over the high rail of the truck. But the velocity of his spittle is not great enough to carry it beyond the wind force of the truck, and it merely flies backward into the eyes and hair of his oldest son. Nostrils flaring and red-faced, Wayne takes the handkerchief his mother has tied around his neck to mop the wet. Blotting pitifully, he works the tired white sheet over his head and face.

— *Fredrick Barton*

6:35 A.M.

IT'S COLD THIS MORNING as I get off work. Eight long hard hours filled with mechanical breakdowns to be repaired. My lower back and right knee are screaming, "Dumbass, why didn't you stay in college instead of coming home to work in a glass factory?" Just another one of life's questions that can't be clearly answered.

I limp to my Harley clad in leather head to toe to help cut the cold biting wind that will soon be surrounding me. I straddle my iron beast and stand her up. Ignition on, gas on, choke on, and start. The big V-twin engine roars to life; it's the best sound I've heard all night. Sitting down, I secure my helmet and glasses, pull up the kickstand, drop her in gear, and roar off into the cold early-morning light.

Damn it's cold, damn I'm tired, and damn I hurt. But it's a beautiful morning. The sky is turning a crystal winter blue without a cloud in sight. A couple of vapor trails from high-flying jets streak the sky. The frigid wind is keeping me alert and awake. The vibration of the V-twin engine begins to soothe some of my aches and pains. Ten and a half miles and I'll be home. Home sweet warm home. A hot shower, a cold beer, then crawl into bed beside my warm sleeping wife for a few hours of broken and painful sleep just to get up and do it all over again tonight.

I head west on I-20 then turn east on I-220, leaving Shreveport behind me. Six and a half miles and I'll be home. The rising sun hasn't appeared over the tops of the pine trees that line the interstate. I ride along in their cold shadows until I reach the bridge over Cross Lake. Now I'm in open sunshine and the temperature rises just enough to notice now that I'm over the open water of the lake. Three and a half miles and I'll be home. Home sweet warm home. A hot shower, a cold beer, then crawl into bed beside my warm sleeping wife for a few hours of broken and painful sleep just to get up and do it all over again tonight.

I'm too tired to appreciate the beauty of this Northwest Louisiana winter morning. Cross Lake's dam is to my right with its trains atop it going into and out of the KCS rail yard. Behind the dam on the horizon is the skyline of downtown Shreveport, Independence Stadium, and the three smokestacks of Libbey Glass where I work, all silhouetted by the rising morning sun. There are scattered areas of wispy vapor rising from the lake. In some places it is thicker and rises slightly higher than the light poles on the bridge. All I notice is the cold wind in my face and the seemingly endless ribbon of concrete ahead of me pointing the way home. Two and a half miles and I'll be home.

But something different catches my attention. Just ahead to my left, about fifty yards west of the bridge is a large black bird soaring upward out of the mist. It is flying away from me, heading west, and begins to circle. I think to myself, "What the hell is a buzzard doing circling over open water?" As it banks in a slow circle toward me now, the sun gleams off its massive wings and I see it is not black but brown, with a white head and tail feathers.

It's an eagle! A mature and magnificent American bald eagle! My favorite of all God's creatures! I've been collecting eagle figures and statues for years. I slow down and come to stop on the shoulder of the bridge to witness and appreciate this rare, once-in-a-lifetime opportunity. This eagle is one of only a handful that migrates this far south and I am allowed to see it!

The wind from passing motorists rocks me on my Harley but I don't notice. My eyes, thoughts, and heart are as one, fully focused on this beautiful, magnificent animal. As it circles it climbs higher. I wonder if it has prey in its sight. A duck, a pigeon, or a fish too close to the surface of the water? Or is it simply there by coincidence, showing off all its splendor and beauty to a weary American blue-collar factory worker on his way home from work? I like to think the latter.

It breaks out of its climbing orbit and flies away to the west. Goodbye! Thank you for showing off for me! Thank you for making me stop to appreciate life's simple, beautiful treasures!

I start my bike and wait for the traffic to clear so I can finish my journey home. It's still cold but I'm not as tired and hurting as I was just a minute ago. Then I notice, to the east, two B-52s circling their home base at Barksdale AFB in Bossier City.

What an amazing coincidence! There for me to witness was the bold, proud symbol of our American freedoms flying on feathered wings. And in the east, in the air at the same time separated by just a few miles, flying on metal wings were the bold, proud defenders of our American freedoms!

I re-enter the traffic to go home. Two more miles and I'll be home. Home sweet *free* home. A hot shower, a cold beer, then slip into bed beside my warm sleeping wife for a few hours of unbroken and peaceful sleep, thankful for the opportunity and ability to do it all over again tonight.

A minute is all it took to change my day.

— Bobby D. Pierce

6:36 A.M.

THE BIKE PATH THAT HE HAS FOLLOWED at water's edge along the southern shore of Lake Pontchartrain stops abruptly at the marshes of St. Charles Parish. Across a swollen canal, thick plugs of swamp grass rise up in little islands that stretch off into the lake all the way to the horizon.

Having gone as far as he can go, the cyclist turns his bike back toward the city. He had not expected to make it to the end of the path, which is littered with the flotsam of the week's storms. He has had to pick his way among bloated redfish seething with flies, shattered branches, and shards of broken bottles strewing the path. The stiff wind he felt at his back out of the east had pushed the lake up over the asphalt bike path in several spots; the cyclist had been forced to coast through the deep puddles holding up his legs like two tusks beneath the handlebars. At times, his spinning wheels ground to a halt in the thick silt deposited by the tides. Mostly, though, he has chased the long shadow cast ahead of him, the helmeted head wobbling on the sharp plane of his shoulders like an egg teetering on a table.

Now he is at the end of civilization. Twenty-five yards away behind the dense forest that has sprouted on the batture between the levee and the lake, watery land waits to be parceled out to young families moving to the outskirts of New Orleans. But for the moment, the muddy waste is home only to snakes, muskrats, and nesting birds. The cyclist is all alone.

Twisting a blue bottle out of its frame, he squirts water into one cheek and slowly swallows. As he straddles his bike, squinting into the huge sun that lies as bright on the lake as in the sky, the wind riffles his loose shirt. Bending down, he plucks a few blades of grass from a crack in the asphalt and tosses them into the air. The breeze carries them over his shoulder and into the canal. He sighs. Getting home will be hard work in this wind.

His foot twists the pedals half a turn. Leaning on the upper one, he feels the lower rise against his foot. He shifts his weight.

Soon he is in the upper gears, struggling against the gusting wind. On the trip out, except for birdcalls and the wheezing of the tires against the path, the morning had been silent; now the roar of the wind into which he bends blasts the cyclist. The racket annoys him, and the knobs of the skull behind his ears grow sore from the chill still on the breeze.

The wind suddenly dies as the bicycle follows the path through a brake of bamboo that juts some distance out into the lake, forming a little pond. Though choppy brown waves break upon the outer walls of bamboo, the water of the pond is utterly still. A huge egret poises in the shallows, its perfectly white feathers brilliant in the sunlight. A few yards away, a swarm of green and black turtles huddles on a half-submerged tree trunk.

The cyclist checks his watch. He still has a long way to go, and against the wind it may take him an extra hour to get home. The woman who by now has awakened and is drinking the coffee he has left for her will certainly be angry if he is an hour late. He will have to hurry — wind or no wind.

— *John Biguenet*

6:40 A.M.

SHORTLY AFTER DAWN. St. Charles and Louisiana. Ash Wednesday. A thumbprint of ash on the foreheads of faithful and unfaithful. No ash at all on the streets, what with the detritus from the last parades having been swept the night before. McDonald's flinging open its doors for the early-morning regulars. Bundles of *Times-Picayunes* being dumped at the front of K&B. A Bultman's van just arriving with a newly departed. And on the neutral ground a small elderly black gentleman in brown suit with white shirt and wrinkled tie. He's dancing slowly, carefully, finely, to a band that only he can hear. On top of his brown felt hat there's a glass of water.

—William Griffin

AFTERWORDS

O.J. Frederic
Highway 931
Gonzales, Louisiana

February 10, 2006

Louisiana in Words
Attention: Joshua Clark

Dear Mr. Clark:

One minute and one page is definitely not enough time and space to relate any event in Louisiana that would adequately portray our people's backgrounds, heritage and traditions. However, since time and space is limited, I will best describe one of the long standing traditions of the people of Gonzales and the surrounding areas with one word—JAMBALAYA. That's right, JAMBALAYA! If you're from New Orleans or have been around there for a while, I am sure that you know what that is. But, if you don't know, please let me try to explain it.

It is very difficult to put into words what JAMBALAYA is. Basically, it is a delicious Cajun/Creole food dish made from a mixture of meat, rice and seasonings. JAMBALAYA is a name derived from the Spanish word, "Jamon," meaning ham and found its way into Cajun cooking in the late 1700s. Thus, the meat used in its preparation is normally pork and/or pork sausage. But, other meats can be used; such as chicken, wild game, crawfish, shrimp or just about any thing else that the cook can get his hands on. It is economical to prepare and can be cooked in a small pot indoors or a large pot outdoors. In and around the Gonzales area, JAMBALAYA is a common meal at fairs, rallies, weddings, family reunions, benefits and other similar affairs. On June 10, 1968, John J. McKeithen, then Governor of Louisiana, proclaimed Gonzales, Louisiana as "The Jambalaya Capital of the World."

There, you have it; the grammatical definition of the word, JAMBALAYA. But, to me, JAMBALAYA is not just a delicious concoction of meat and rice. It is far more than that. Because it is so economical to prepare and so filling, it brings people together to pass a good time at a very modest cost. It is about hunters around an open camp fire discussing the day's hunt while JAMBALAYA is being prepared with some of the day's kill. It is about a group of people gladly preparing JAMBALAYA which will be sold to benefit some needy person. It is about some mother of a poor family, struggling to feed her hungry children the cheapest and best way she knows how; with a LUNCHMEAT JAMBALAYA. It can be and is enjoyed by the rich as well as the poor. Around here, and the surrounding areas, JAMBALAYA is not just a word or a meal; it's an INSTITUTION. To try to describe Louisiana traditions without mentioning JAMBALAYA would be like trying to describe Paris France without mentioning the Louvre or the Eiffel Tower.

That's it for now. Good luck with your venture. Laissez les bons temps rouler!

O.J. Frederic

Rebekah Markel
8 years old
Scott, LA
3-8-06

Maddi's Mudbug Mama

Louisiana crawfish is so juicy and tastes wonderful. There are crawfish big and small. When Maddi, a Louisiana girl born in Lafayette, eats crawfish, she usually eats the tail. But sometimes she eats other parts like the huge claws. When Maddi is waiting for her crawfish, she is dying to have these wonderful, red creatures (crawfish). Before she devours her crawfish, she cracks open the shell and dips it in her special sauce, which is a mixture of salt, ranch dressing, seasoning, and another ingredient I will not mention. After she swallows the tail, she scrapes the claw meat off of the bone and then licks her fingers. She says after she gulps down her crawfish, she sits back with a satisfied smile.

Linda L. Boudoin
Jeanerette, La.
February 14, 2006

Louisiana in Words

My name is Linda. I live in Jeanerette, Louisiana. Today's date is February 14, 2006. The time is 6:20 a.m.

I am an ordinary housewife. I have been married to "Allen" for twenty-four years. Our five children are grown. Our sixth and youngest is fifteen.

Cody is not supposed to need my nudging to get up for school. Just last night he promised to limit himself on the computer. I'll still get out of bed at around 11:00 p.m. to turn off his desk light. The days are dwindling. I won't have this small chore much longer.

He is thrilled to have his learner's permit. He drives his dad's first new vehicle, a 1996 Chevy pickup truck. The paint is peeling, where it used to be white. But, Cody thinks it's the perfect truck for "mudding."

As I look back at the forty-two years that I've spent on this earth, I can laugh. I laugh because I can't cry anymore. To watch my children struggle, then succeed . . . is pure joy! The other side is at times unbearable.

INDEX